100 Best Full-Size

Quilt Blocks & Borders

Phyllis Dobbs

Mimi Shimp

Lucie Sinkler

Retta Warehime

Publications International, Ltd.

DESIGNERS:

Phyllis Dobbs (Fresh from the Garden) is the author of *Dimensional Quilts* and *Fun with Flannel.* Her designs
appear in many books and magazines. She teaches and demonstrates quilt and stitch techniques
at local and national levels and has designed a whimsical fabric collection for Hancock Fabrics. Dobbs
is a member of the Society of Craft Designers.

Mimi Shimp (Hearts, Bars & Shooting Stars) offers quilting classes both nationally and in Las Vegas,
where she owns her own quilting business, Quiltime. She is the author of *Twelve Days of Christmas, Stolen Moments,*
The Garden Club, Hearthside Hangings, More Hearthside Hangings, and numerous patterns. Her quilts have been
featured in *Quilting Today* and *The Quilter* magazines. Shimp designs
and makes quilt samples for quilting fabric manufacturers.

Lucie Sinkler (Traditional Treasures) is a versatile designer who specializes in both quilted and knitted projects.
Her designs have appeared in national magazines including *Vogue, Christmas Crafts,* and
Knitting Made Easy. Her focus for this book was on traditional patchwork designs.

Retta Warehime (Country Cupboard) is the author of *Snuggle Up, Patchwork Memories, Quilting*
Your Just Desserts, Farm House Quilts, and many other titles. She has taught piecing and quilting
techniques for 24 years and has been designing and publishing quilt patterns for 18 years through her company,
Sew Cherished. Warehime has published more than 200 quilt designs and is currently designing and
publishing quilts for fabric company Web sites.

ILLUSTRATIONS:
Connie Formby

QUILT BLOCK AND BORDER PHOTOGRAPHY:
© Deborah Van Kirk

SAMPLER QUILT PHOTOGRAPHY:
Brian Warling/Warling Studios

Louis Weber, CEO
Publications International, Ltd.
7373 North Cicero Avenue
Lincolnwood, Illinois 60712

Permission is never granted for commercial purposes.

Manufactured in China.

8 7 6 5 4 3 2 1

ISBN: 1-4127-1044-8

Library of Congress Control Number: 2004118173

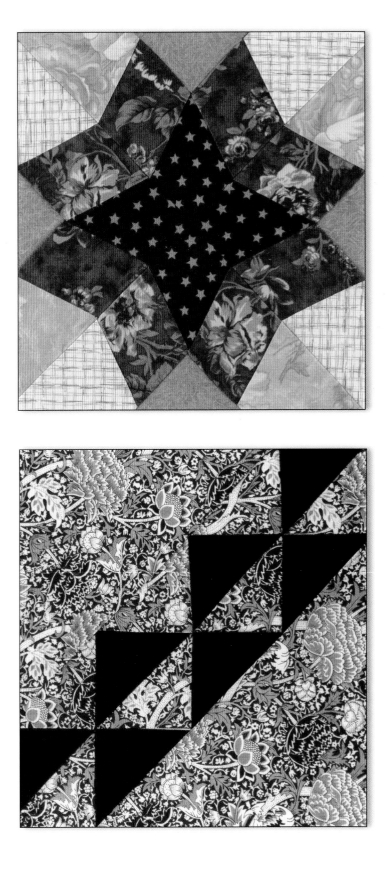

Contents

6 ## Hearts, Bars & Shooting Stars
Virginia Reel • Twisted Star • True Lover's Knot • Sweet Clover •
Sun Rays • Shooting Star • Ohio Snowflake • Judy in Arabia •
Heart Wreath • Girl's Joy • Pride of the Bride • Friendship Star •
Emily's Heart • Double T • Diamond Star • Cupid's Own •
Crazy Patch • Heart's Delight • Borrow and Return •
Eight-Pointed Star

48 ## Country Cupboard
Windblown Puzzle • Watermelon • Teapot • Twelve Triangles •
Handweave • Honey Pot • Home Sweet Home • Garden of Eden •
Hourglass • Churn Dash • Rooster • Heart Can • Double Heart •
Attic Window • Cherry Basket • Apple Pie • Grandma's Bowls •
City Streets • Chimneys and Cornerstones • Apple Cider

90 ## Traditional Treasures
Traditional Fan • Stained Glass • Square upon Square • Palm Tree •
Ohio Star • London Square • Log Cabin • Kaleidoscope •
Friendship Star (Variation) • Four Corner Flowers • Flying Geese
(Variation) • Double Pinwheel • Cross • Friendship Circle •
Chinese Fan • Chain (Variation) • Card Trick • Basket •
Album Block • Rail Fence

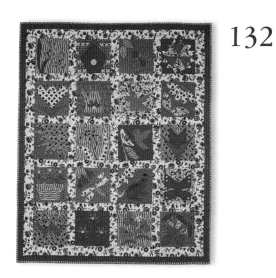

132 Fresh from the Garden

Wayward Daisy • Watering Can • Trumpeting Tulip • Sunshine Day • Flying High • Sweet Nectar • Summer Sunflower • Pretty Maids • My Favorite Flower • Fly Away Ladybug! • Peeping Out • Inching Along • Johnny-Jump-Ups • Fluttering by Butterfly • Gossamer Wings • Garden Queen Iris • Good Morning Glory • Bloom Well Groomed • Birdhouse Treasure • Pretty Bird

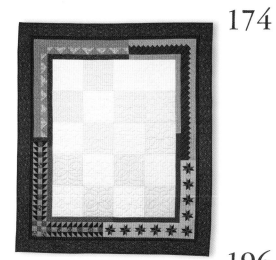

174 Borders

Block Leaf • Rambling Leaves • Double Picture Frame • Flowers and More • Blocks and Bars • Bricks • Piano Keys • Rickrack • Flying Geese • Scalloped • Stop Sign • Hearts • Churn Dash • Bars and Blocks • Diamond Star Squares • Jagged Edge • Sawtooth Square • Braided • Eight-Pointed Star • Triangles

196 Start a Quilting Adventure!

206 Blocks and Borders Index

208 Resource Directory

Hearts, Bars & Shooting Stars

♥ ■ ★ ■ ♥

Who doesn't love hearts? And for that matter, who doesn't love stars? Add a few bars to either, and you're sure to have a hit. Quilters have used these themes for as many years as there have been quilters. So here are some favorite old blocks along with some new twists. Whether you're into traditional or more modern, you're sure to find something in this chapter that will get your creativity working overtime. Anyone who receives a quilt from you will know how much heart you put into it. So shoot for the stars, and get quilting!

Virginia Reel

BLOCK
Cut

A: Cut 8, and cut 4 from contrasting fabric. B: Cut 4. C: Cut 4. D: Cut 16. E: Cut 16. (Note: Mark outside edge of template B, C, D, E; place this edge on straight of grain when cutting.)

Stitch

Stitch A to contrast A, then sew on another A (sidebar); make 4. Stitch D to E; make 16. Stitch 4 DE's together to make a square (small pinwheel); make 4. Stitch B to C; make 4. Stitch BC's together to make a square (large pinwheel). Stitch a small pinwheel to each end of a sidebar; make 2. Stitch sidebar to each side of large pinwheel. Sew rows together to complete square.

TWIRLING TABLE RUNNER

Make 3 blocks. Sew them together, and add sashing, side borders, and large triangles on ends. Finished size is about 39×11 inches.

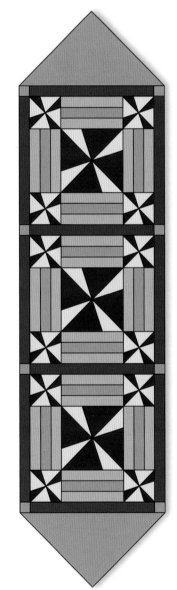

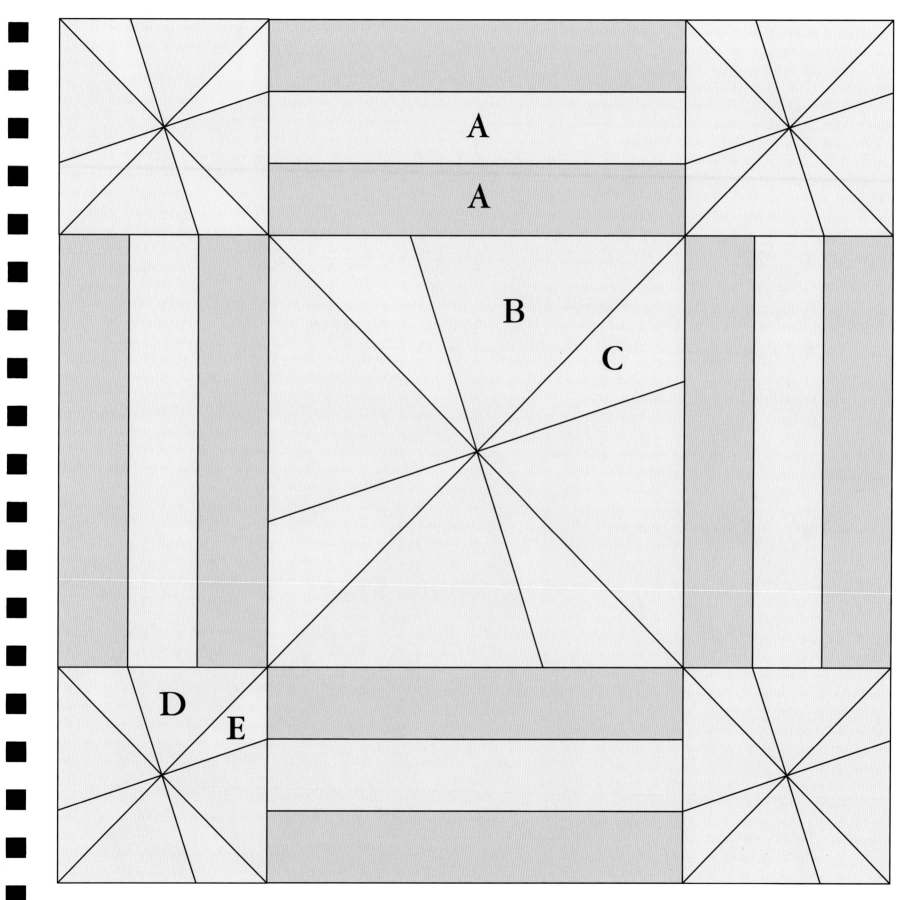

Twisted Star

BLOCK

Cut

A: Cut 4, and cut 4 from reverse pattern and contrasting fabric. B: Cut 4 (cut on straight of grain where indicated by arrow). C: Cut 1.

Stitch

Stitch A to B, then stitch reverse A to other side of B. Stitch short end of reverse A to short end of A. Make 2. Stitch B to A, then stitch AB to C. Stitch A to other side of C, and stitch B to other side of A. Stitch rows together to complete square.

STARRY QUILT

Make 16 blocks, and stitch them together in 4 rows of 4 blocks. Add border. Finished size is about 40 inches square.

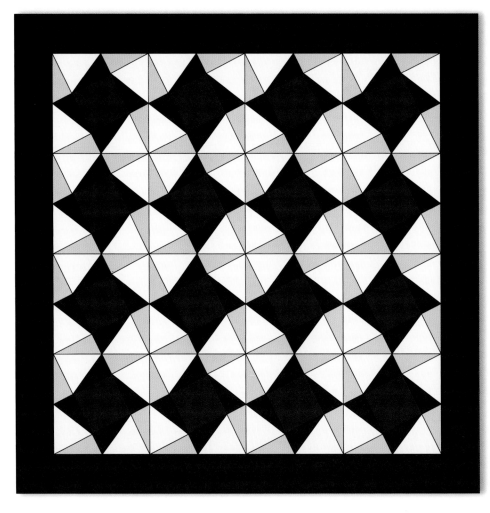

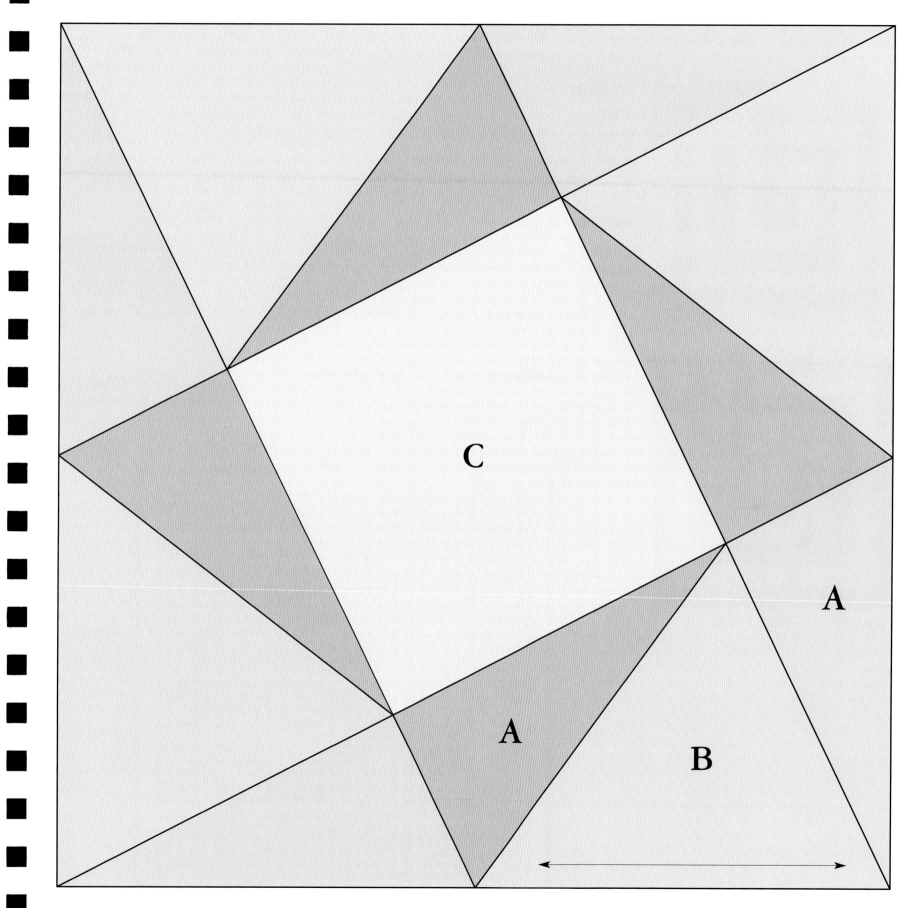

True Lover's Knot

BLOCK

Cut

From background color, cut pieces 1, 5, 6, 8, 9, 12, 14, 16, 17. From main color, cut pieces 2, 3, 4, 7, 10, 11, 13, 15, 18, 19, 20, 21. Piece A: Cut 4 from background color, and cut 4 from main color.

Stitch

At end of piece 9, sew a main A, then a background A. Repeat with piece 12. At end of piece 17, sew a main A, then a background A, then a main A, and finish with a background A. Stitch strips together in number order, placing them as shown on pattern. For example, stitch 2 to top of 1, then stitch 3 to left side of that piece, etc. Continue adding strips until block is complete.

KNOTTED TOGETHER WALL QUILT

Make 36 blocks, and stitch them together in 6 rows of 6 blocks. Add outside borders. Finished size is about 60 inches square.

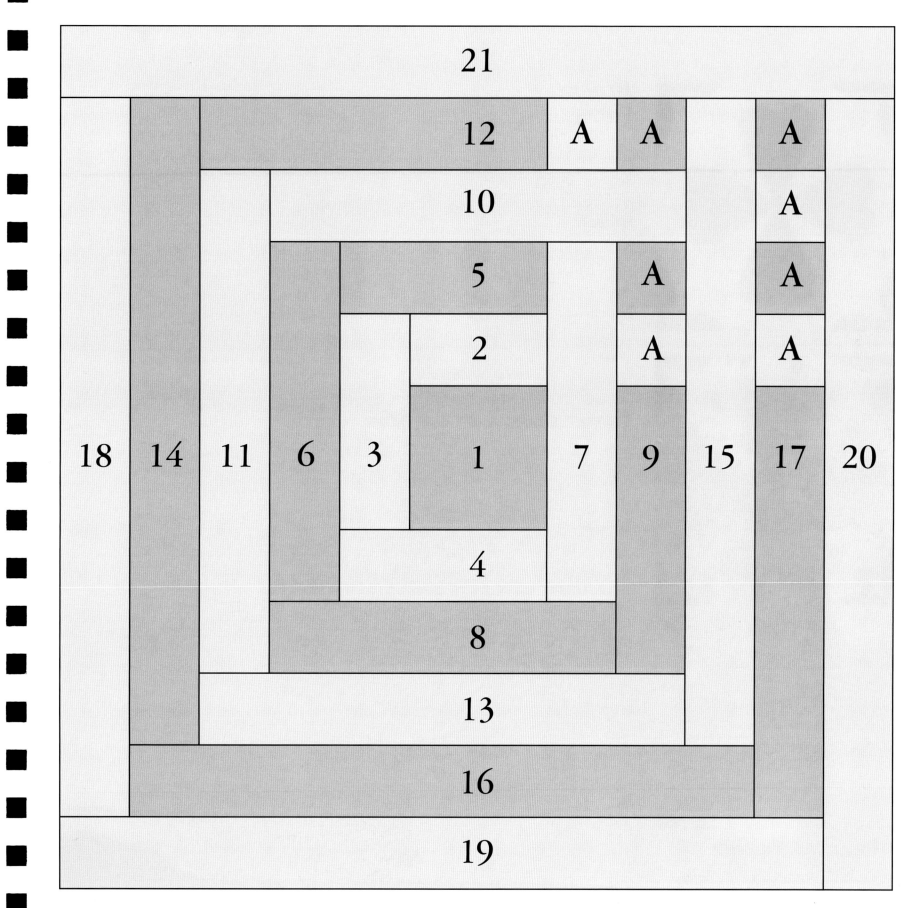

Sweet Clover

BLOCK

Cut

A: Cut 4, and cut 4 from fusible webbing. B: Cut 8, and cut 8 from fusible webbing. C: (This is a 4-inch square.) Cut 1 from 4 similar fabrics. (Variation: Cut background square as 1 piece of fabric.)

Stitch

Sew C's together to make background square. With right side of A to fusible side of webbing A, sew together. Clip curves, and trim seam allowances. Cut a small slit in webbing, and turn. Make 4. Fuse all hearts to middle of background square, with points in middle of square. With right side of B to fusible side of webbing B, sew together along curve only. Clip curves, trim seam allowances, and turn. Make 8. Fuse B's to outside corners of background square. By hand or machine, appliqué all fused pieces using narrow blanket stitch.

IN THE CLOVER PLACE MAT

Make 2 blocks, and stitch them together. Add top and bottom borders. Finished size is about 18×22 inches.

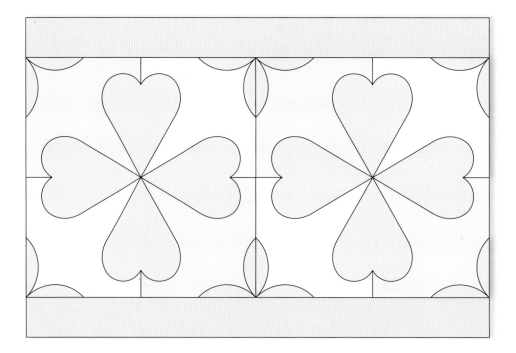

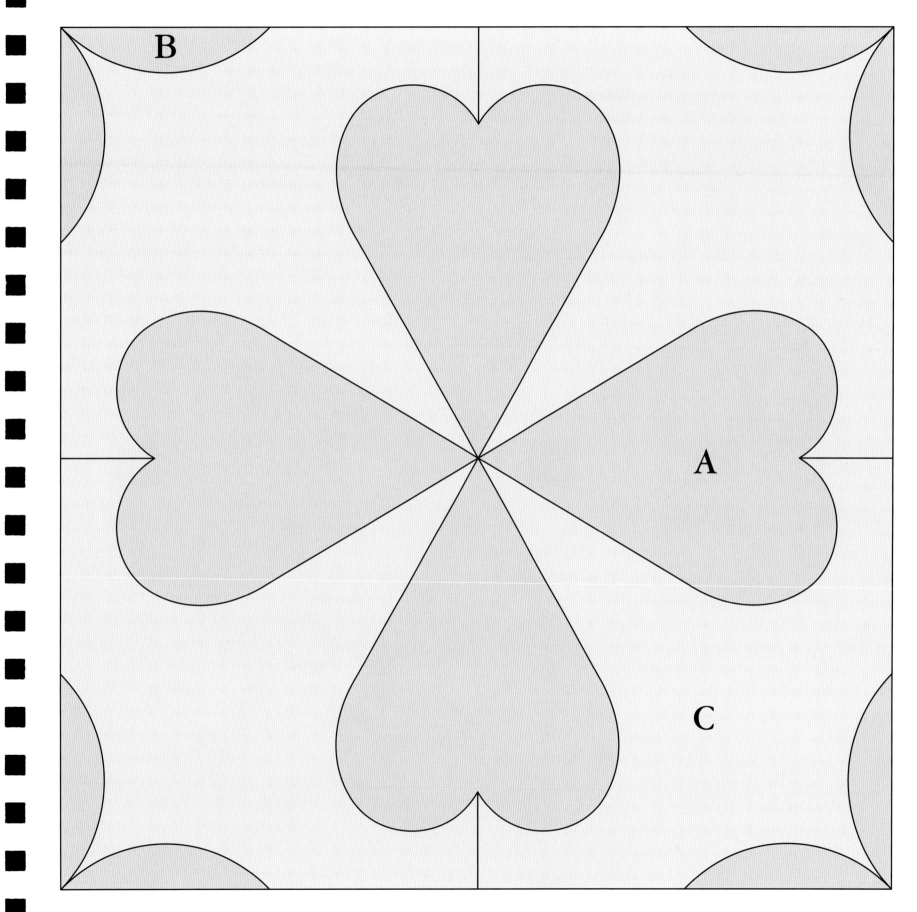

B

A

C

Sun Rays

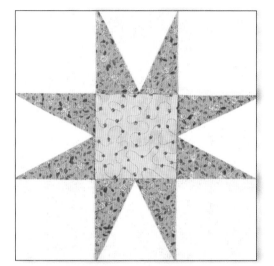

BLOCK
Cut

A: Cut 4, and cut 1 from contrasting fabric. B: Cut 4. C: Cut 4, and cut 4 from reverse pattern.

Stitch

Stitch C to long side of B; stitch reverse C to other long side of B. Make 4. Stitch A to CBC, and stitch A to other side of CBC. Make 2. Stitch CBC to contrast A, with C points directed away from A. Stitch CBC to other side of A, directing C points outward. Sew rows together, with all C points directed outward, to complete block.

SUN SHINING QUILT

Make 5 blocks, and set blocks on point. Cut triangles to fit spaces to make a large square quilt face. Add blocks and bars border (see page 180). Finished size is about 32 inches square.

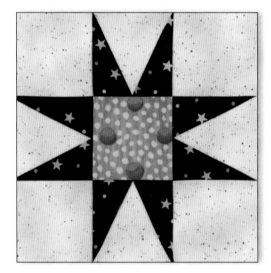

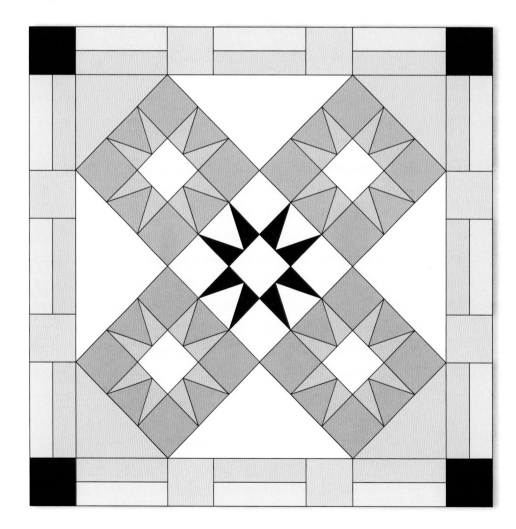

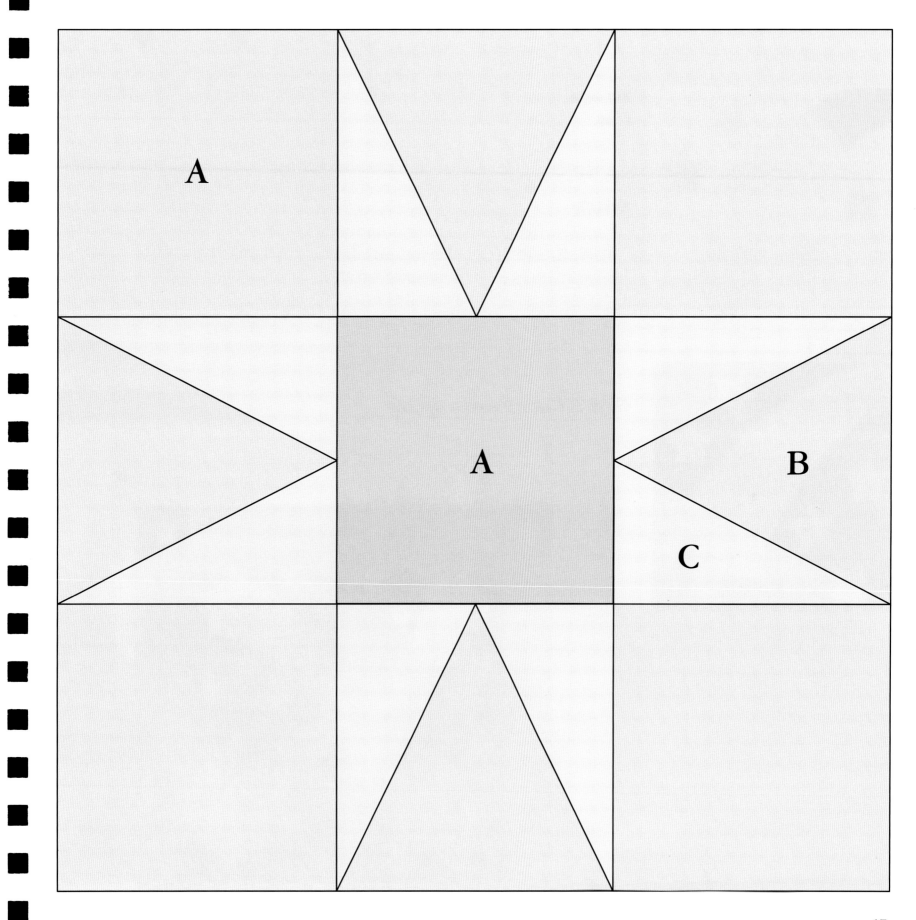

Shooting Star

BLOCK

Cut

Background: Cut 1. A–C: Cut 1 each from different fabrics. D: Cut 1, and cut 1 from fusible webbing. E: Cut 5, and cut 5 from fusible webbing.

Stitch

Stitch A to B, and stitch C to BA (tail). Clip curves. Cut a 5×12-inch piece of fusible webbing. With fusible side of webbing to right side of tail, stitch with a ¼-inch seam allowance on long sides; do not stitch top or bottom. Trim seam allowances, and turn. Trim webbing at bottom and top. Fuse tail to square. Sew webbing to stars, with fusible side of webbing to right side of stars. Clip corners, and trim allowances. Make a slit in webbing, and turn. Fuse stars to square. By hand or machine, appliqué pieces using narrow blanket stitch.

OUR STARS PHOTO QUILT

Following any photo transfer method, transfer photos to stars before appliqué. Make 4 blocks, and sew them together as shown. Add border strips. With a fine-tip permanent marker, write photo names on each star. Finished size is about 26 inches square.

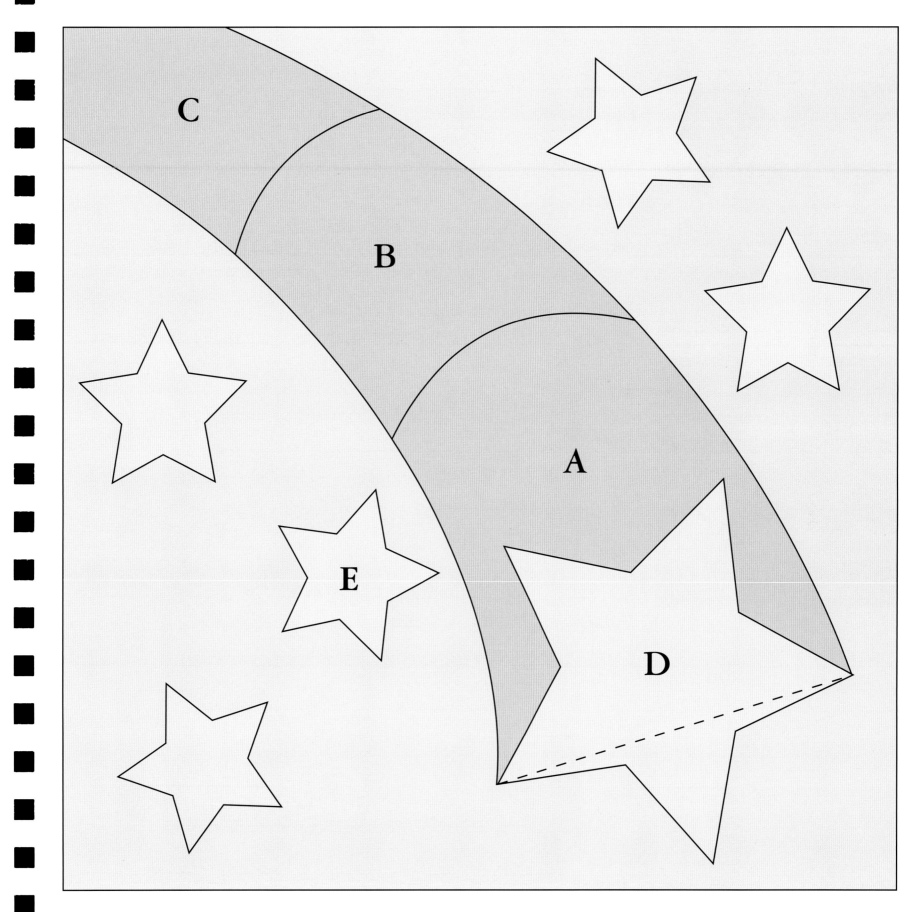

Ohio Snowflake

BLOCK

Cut

A: Cut 4. B: Cut 8, and cut 8 from contrasting fabric. C: Cut 8, and cut 8 from contrasting fabric. D: Cut 1.

Stitch

Stitch B to contrast B; make 8. Stitch BB to A, and stitch BB to other side of A (corner). Make 4. Stitch C to contrast C; make 8. Stitch CC to CC (side); make 4. Stitch corner to side to corner; make 2. Stitch side to D to side. Sew rows together to complete block.

WINTER WONDER WALL HANGING

Make 4 squares, and add sashing and triangles border (see page 195). Finished size is about 27½ inches square.

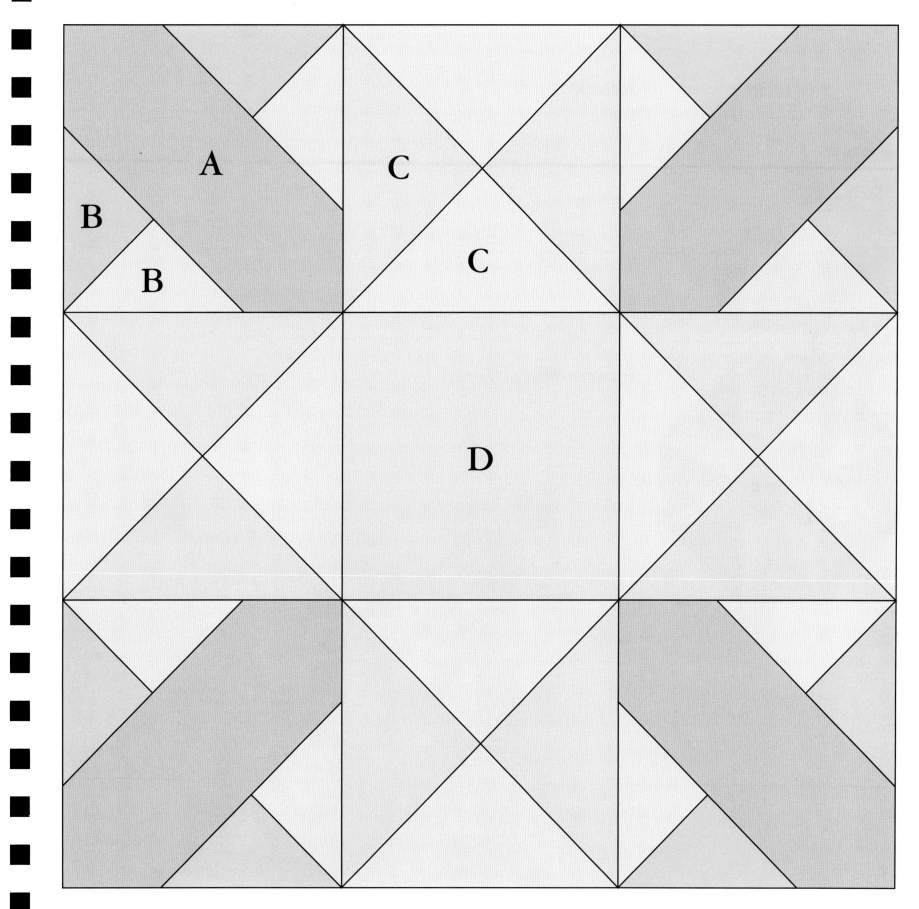

Judy in Arabia

BLOCK
Cut

A: Cut 4, and cut 4 from contrasting fabric. B: Cut 4. C: Cut 4, and cut 4 from reverse pattern. D: Cut 2, and cut 2 from contrasting fabric.

Stitch

Stitch A to contrast A; make 4. Stitch long side of C to B, then stitch reverse C to other long side of B. Make 4. Stitch D to contrast D; make 2. Stitch DD to DD to make center square, matching unlike fabrics. Stitch AA to CBC, then stitch AA to other side of CBC. (Main A's are outside corners.) Make 2. Stitch CBC to center square, with C points directed away from center. Stitch CBC to other side of center square, again directing C points away from center square. Stitch rows together to complete block.

EXOTIC WALL QUILT

Make 4 blocks and 8 CBC blocks. Cut four 3½-inch squares and eight 3½×6½-inch rectangles. Stitch pieces together as shown. Add borders with 4-patch corners. Finished size is about 30 inches square.

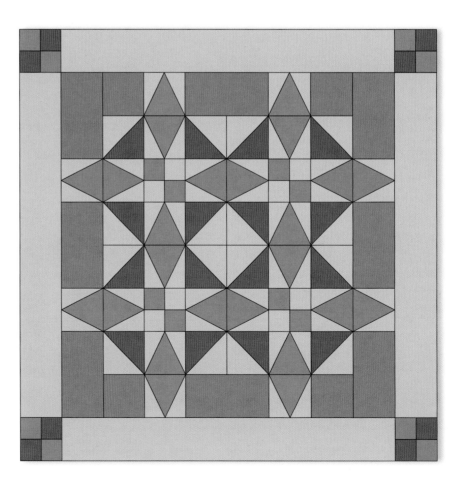

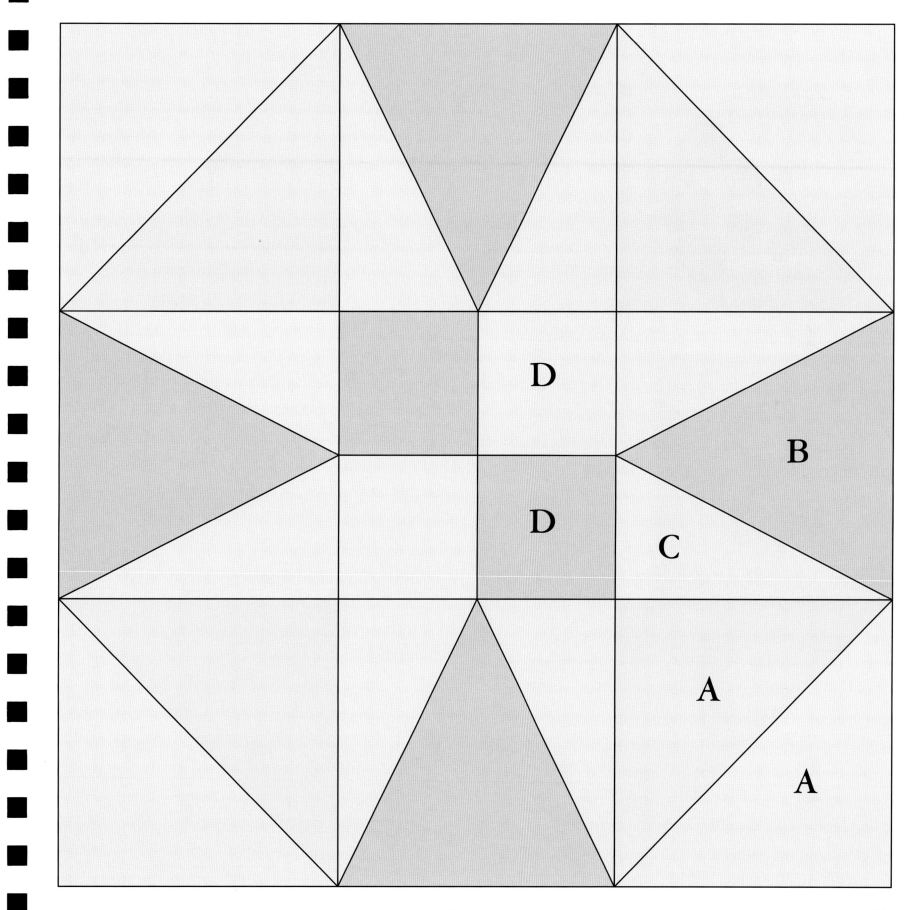

Heart Wreath

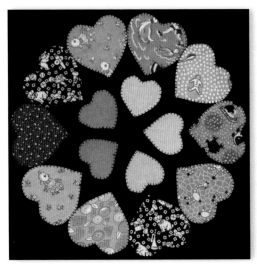

BLOCK

Cut

Background: Cut 1. Large hearts: Cut 10, and cut 10 from fusible webbing. Small hearts: Cut 5, and cut 5 from fusible webbing.

Stitch

Stitch fusible webbing to hearts with fusible side to right side of fabric. Clip curves, and trim seam allowances. Cut a slit in webbing, and turn. Fuse hearts to background square. By hand or machine, appliqué all pieces using narrow blanket stitch.

HEARTS ON YOUR PILLOW

Make 1 block, making background square size to fit pillow form. Add narrow inside border and scalloped border (see page 185). Finished size depends on size of pillow form.

Girl's Joy

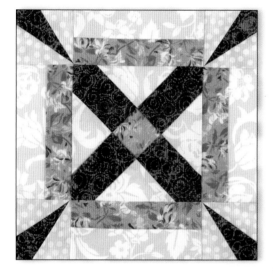

BLOCK

Cut

A: Cut 4, and cut 4 from reverse pattern. B: Cut 4. C: Cut 4. D: Cut 4. E: Cut 1. F: Cut 4, and cut 4 from contrasting fabric.

Stitch

Stitch A to B, then stitch AB to reverse A. Make 4. Stitch C to D, then stitch CD to C. Make 2. Stitch D to E, then stitch DE to D. Stitch CDC to DED, then stitch this piece to CDC (middle square). Stitch F to contrast F; make 4. Stitch ABA to each end of FF; make 2. Stitch FF to either side of middle square. Stitch rows together to complete block.

JOYFUL BED QUILT

Make 12 blocks, and stitch them together in 4 rows of 3 blocks. Make 12 ABA pieces, and piece them in corners of inner border. Add outer border. Finished size is about 34×47 inches.

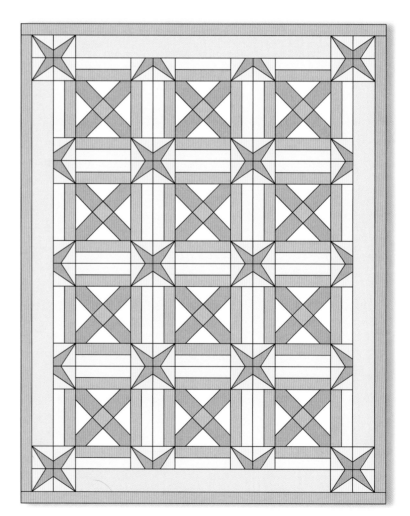

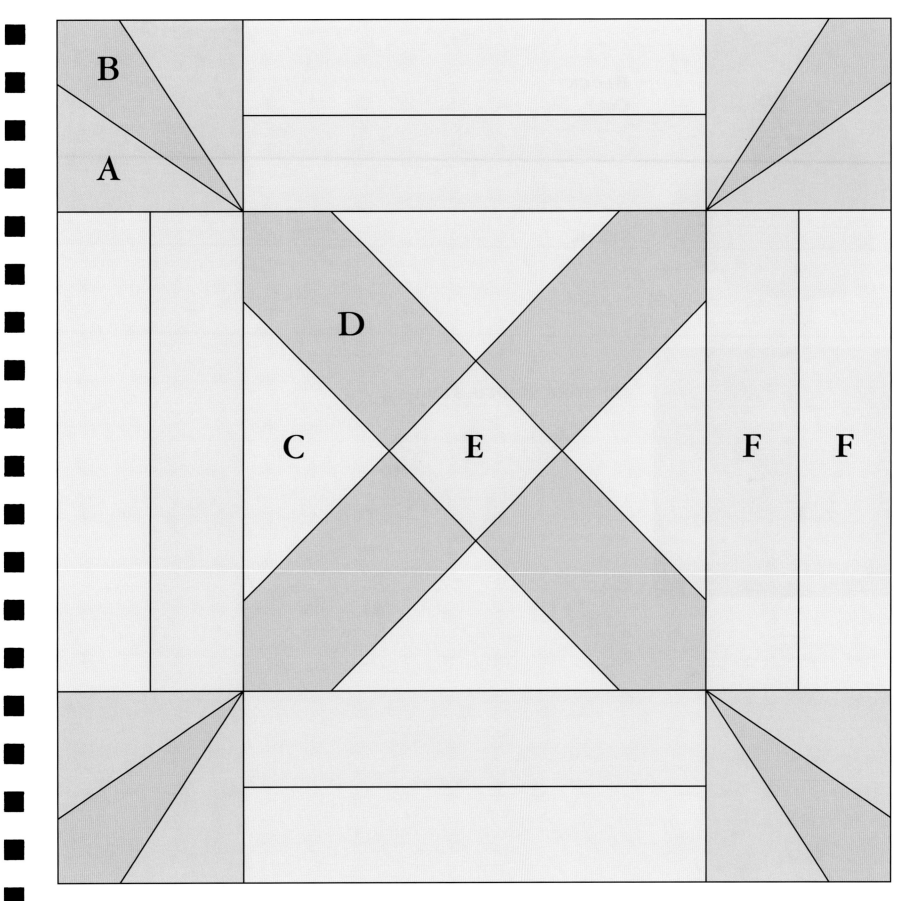

Pride of the Bride

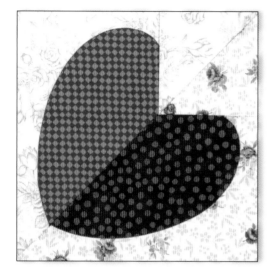

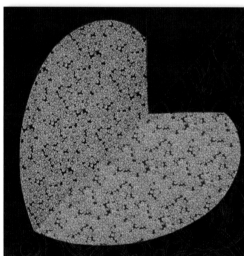

BLOCK
Cut

A: Cut 1, and cut 1 from reverse pattern and contrasting fabric. (These pieces include area under C pieces.) B: Cut 1, and cut 1 from contrasting fabric. C: Cut 1, and cut 1 from fusible webbing; cut 1 from reverse pattern and contrasting fabric, and cut 1 reverse pattern from fusible webbing.

Stitch

Stitch fusible side of webbing to right side of heart along outside edges. Make 2. Clip curves, and trim allowances. Turn. Fuse heart half to A, matching top of heart to notched edge of A. Make 2. Stitch B to top notch of heart/A, matching like fabrics. Make 2. Stitch triangles together, matching heart halves. By hand or machine, appliqué around curve of heart (but not notched edge) using narrow blanket stitch.

MEMORY PHOTO ALBUM

Make 1 block, and add hearts border (see page 187) to fit size of photo album. Finished size depends on size of album.

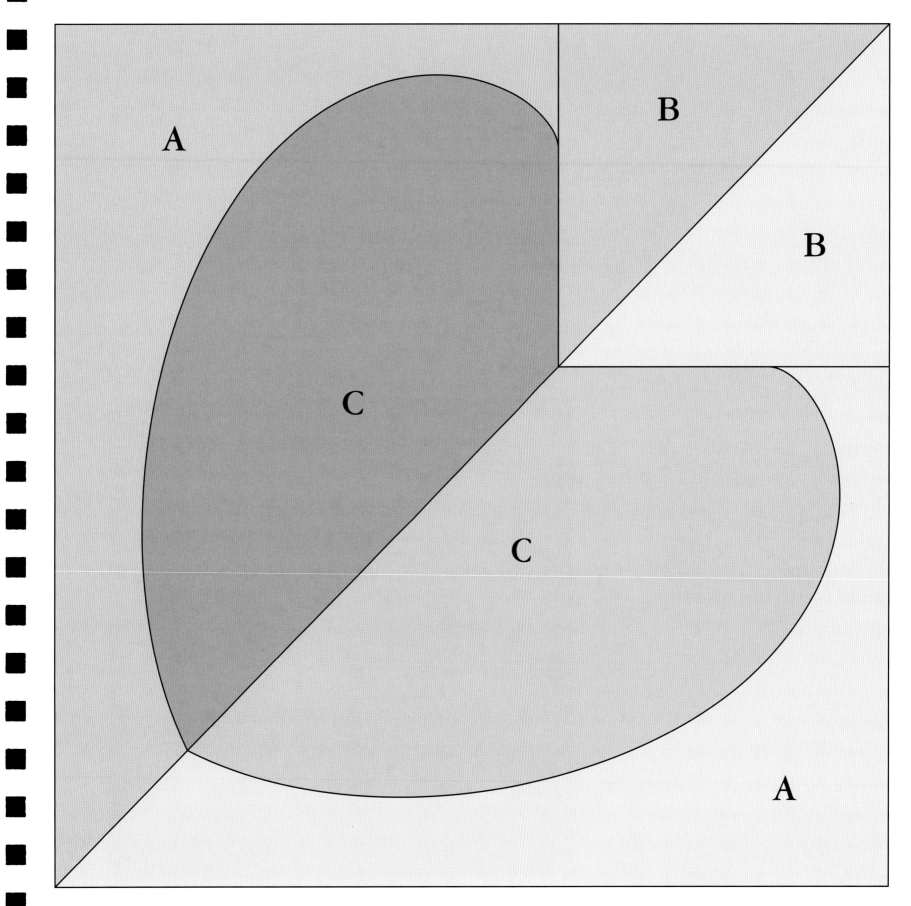

Friendship Star

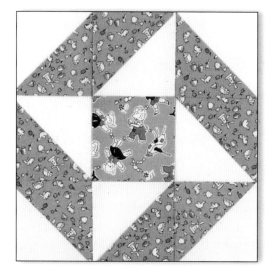

BLOCK

Cut

A: Cut 8, and cut 8 from background fabric. B: Cut 1.

Stitch

Stitch A to background A; make 8. Stitch an AA to AA, matching fabrics. Stitch AA to other side, matching unlike fabrics. Make 2. Stitch AA to B, matching unlike fabrics, then stitch AA to other side of B, matching unlike fabrics. Stitch rows together to complete block.

FRIENDSHIP QUILT

Make 16 blocks, and sew them together in 4 rows of 4 blocks. Add braided border (see page 193). Finished size is about 43 inches square.

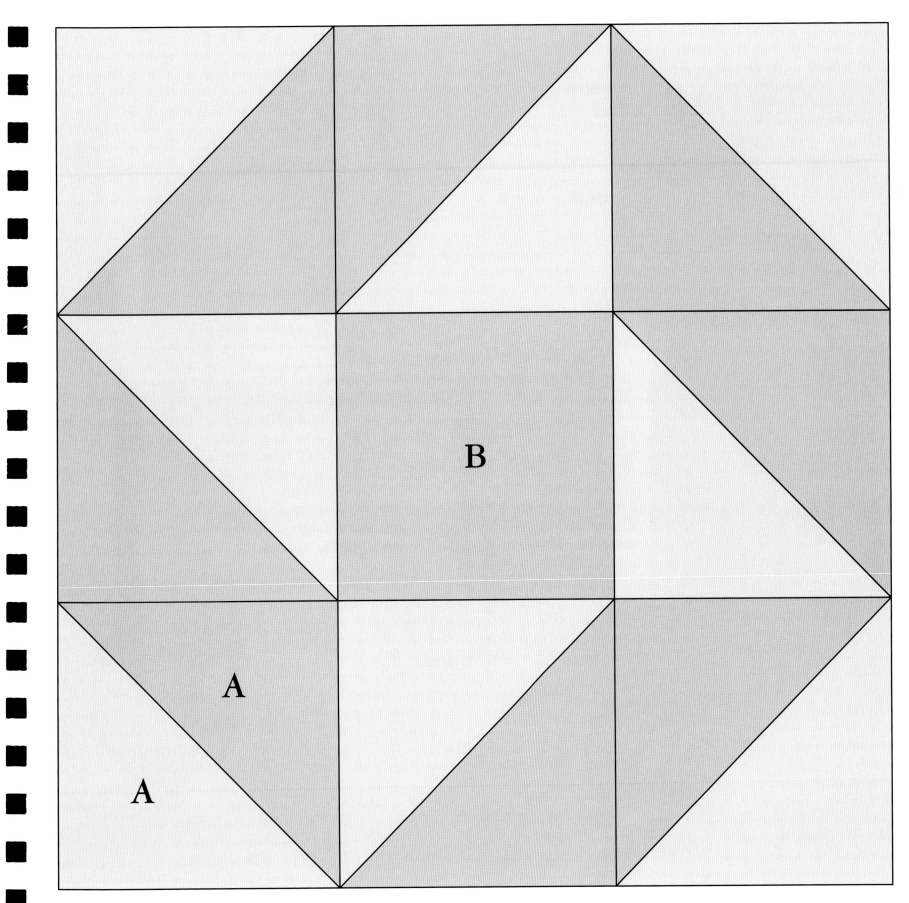

Emily's Heart

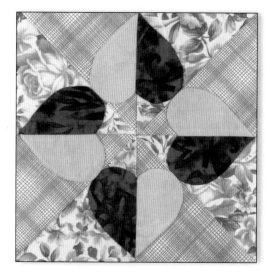

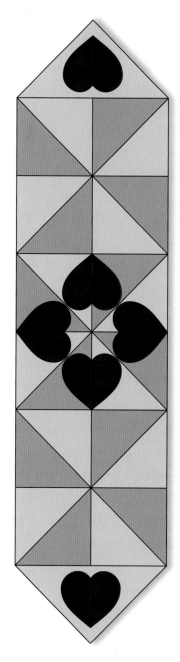

BLOCK

Cut

A: Cut 4, and cut 4 from contrasting fabric. (These pieces include area under heart appliqué.) B: Cut 4, and cut 4 from reverse pattern and contrasting fabric.

Stitch

Stitch A to contrast A; make 4. Stitch AA's together to make a pinwheel square. Stitch B to contrast B along heart middle; make 4. Trace and cut fusible webbing heart; make 4. With fusible side of webbing to right side of heart, sew webbing to heart; make 4. Clip curves, and trim seam allowances. Cut a small slit in webbing, and turn. Place hearts so center seam is on a horizontal or vertical seam of pinwheel. Fuse hearts to pinwheel. By hand or machine, appliqué all pieces using narrow blanket stitch.

EMILY'S TABLE RUNNER

Make 3 blocks but only 1 block with appliqué hearts. Stitch blocks together in a row, with hearts block in center. Add large triangles to each end, and appliqué a heart on each. Finished size is about 37×9 inches.

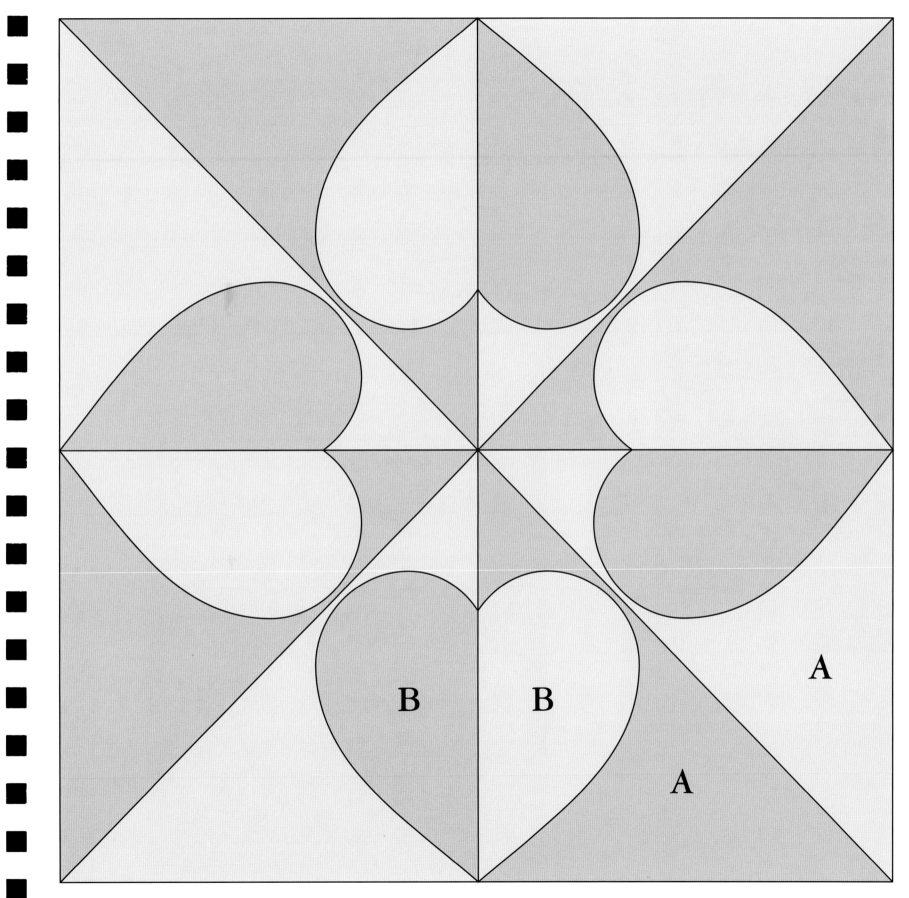

Double T

BLOCK

Cut

A: Cut 8. B: Cut 4, and cut 4 reverse pattern. C: Cut 4. D: Cut 4. E: Cut 4. F: Cut 1.

Stitch

Stitch A to B; make 8. Stitch AB to C, then stitch ABC to reverse AB (T piece); make 4. Stitch E to T piece, then stitch E to other side of T piece; make 2. Stitch T piece to F, then stitch other T piece to other side of F. Stitch rows together, then stitch D pieces to top of each T piece to complete block.

DOUBLY LOVELY QUILT

Make 42 squares, and sew them together in 7 rows of 6 blocks. Add a double border and block corners. Finished size is about 69×60 inches.

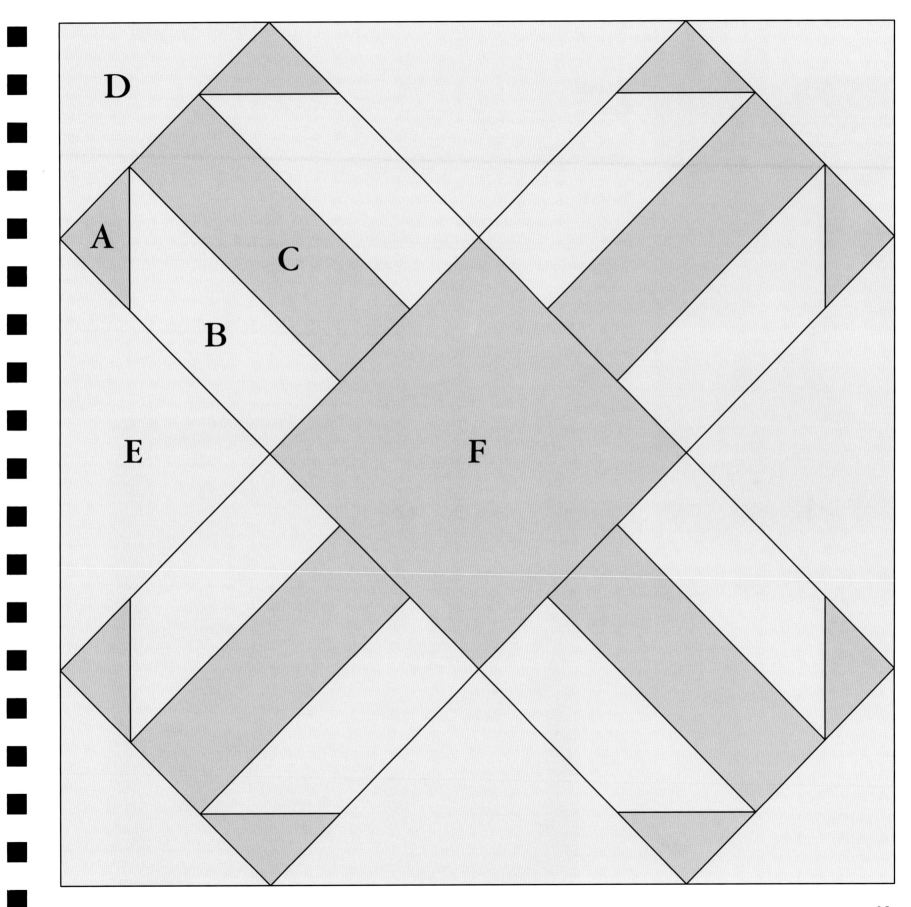

Diamond Star

BLOCK

Cut

A: Cut 4. B: Cut 4, and cut 4 reverse pattern. C: Cut 4, and cut 4 from reverse pattern and contrasting fabric. D: Cut 4.

Stitch

Stitch B to A, and stitch reverse B to other side of BA. Make 4. Stitch C to BAB, and stitch contrast C to other side of CBAB. Make 4. Stitch D between B and reverse B; make 4. Stitch triangles together, matching points of A's, to complete block.

DIAMOND STAR QUILT

Make 16 blocks, and stitch them together in 4 rows of 4 blocks. Add a double border. Finished size is about 42 inches square.

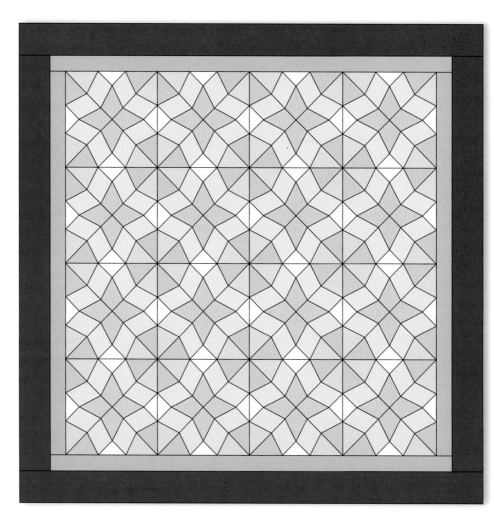

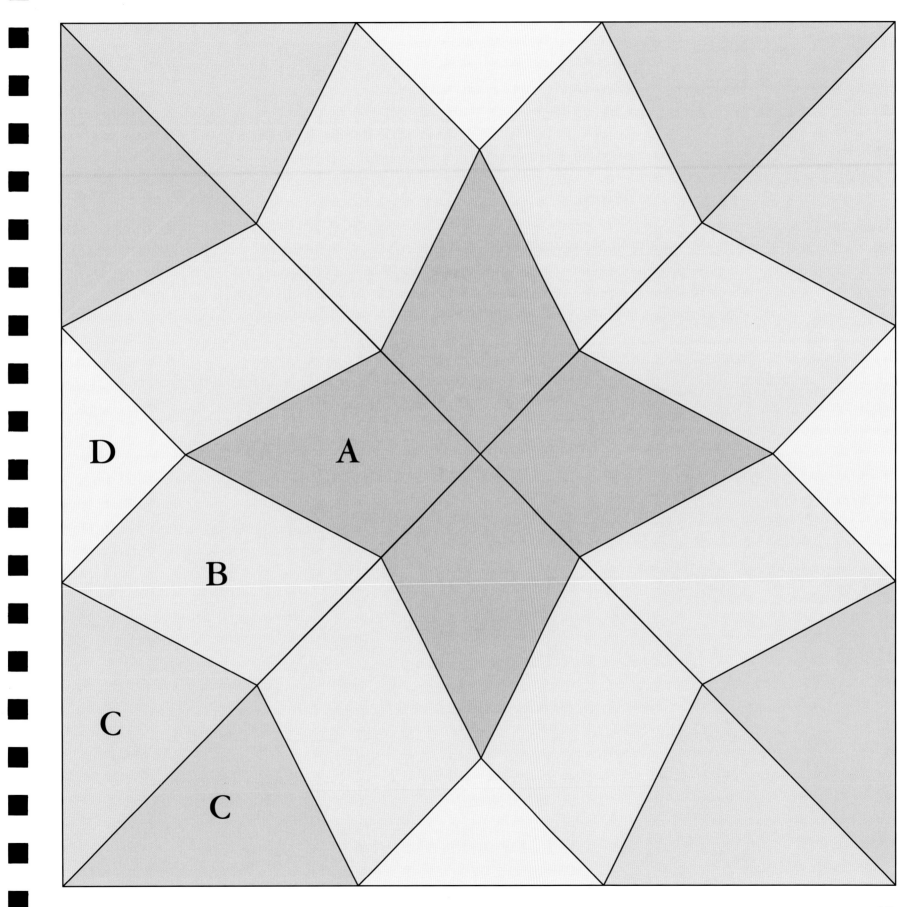

Cupid's Own

BLOCK

Cut

A: Cut 8. B: Cut 4 (pieces include area under hearts). C: Cut 4. D: Cut 1. E: Cut 4, and cut 4 from fusible webbing.

Stitch

Stitch A to B, then stitch AB to A. Make 4. Stitch ABA to C, then stitch ABA to other side of C. Make 2. Stitch C to D, then stitch CD to C. Stitch rows together to form block. Sew fusible side of webbing to right side of heart; make 4. Clip curves, and trim seam allowances. Cut small slit in webbing, and turn. Fuse hearts to block. By hand or machine, appliqué hearts using narrow blanket stitch.

CUPID'S OWN WALL HANGING

Make 9 blocks, and stitch them together in 3 rows of 3 blocks. Add a double border. Finished size is about 36 inches square.

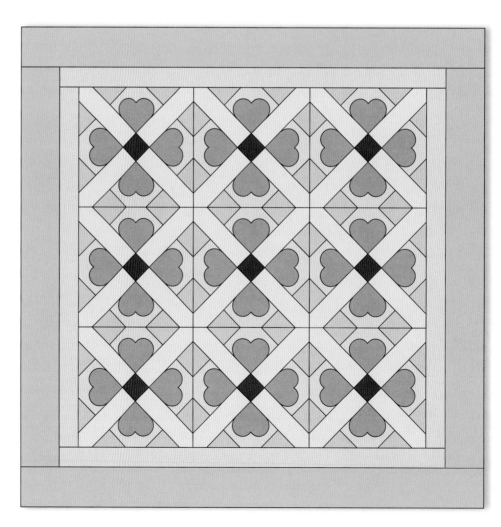

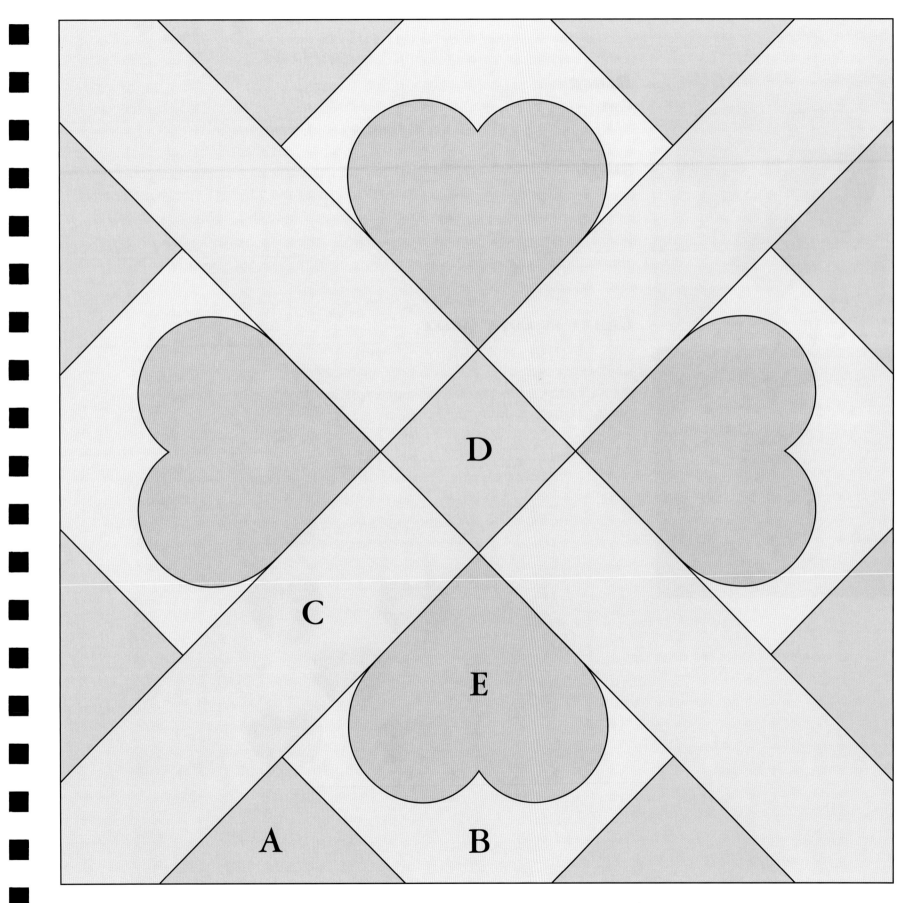

Crazy Patch

BLOCK

Cut

Background: Cut 1. A–I: Cut 1 each from a few different fabrics.

Stitch

Stitch A to B, then stitch AB to C. Stitch D to E, then stitch DE to F. Stitch G to H, then stitch GH to I. Stitch rows together to form heart. Cut fusible webbing heart. Stitch fusible side of webbing to right side of heart. Clip curves, and trim seam allowance. Cut a small slit in webbing, and turn heart. Fuse heart in place on background. By hand or machine, appliqué heart using narrow blanket stitch.

CRAZY IN LOVE QUILT

Make 5 heart blocks, placing hearts on diagonals. Cut triangles to fit spaces to make a large square quilt face. Add patchwork inner and outer borders. Use background material for middle border. Quilt small patchwork hearts where indicated in illustration. Finished size is about 38 inches square.

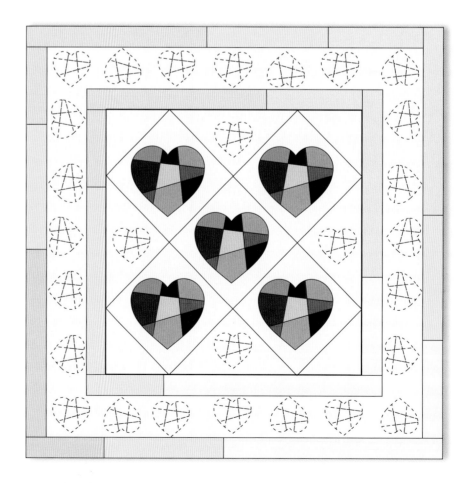

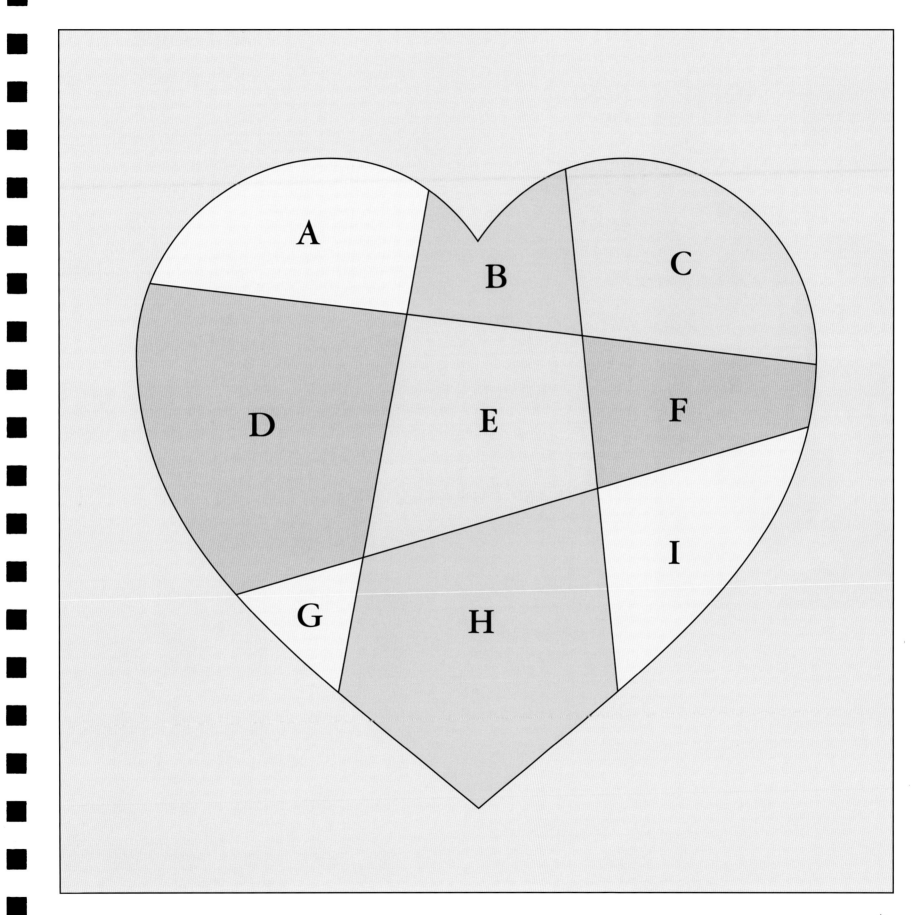

Heart's Delight

BLOCK
Cut

(For pieces A, B, and C, choose 2 color palettes.) A–C: Cut 4, and cut 4 from contrasting fabric. D: Cut 4 (pieces include area under appliquéd pieces). E: Cut 1, and cut 1 from fusible webbing.

Stitch

Sew A to bottom of B, then stitch AB to bottom of C. Make 8 (make 4 in 1 color palette and 4 in the other, keeping 2 sets of colors consistent). Trace ABC piece on fusible webbing 8 times; cut out. Sew fusible side of webbing to right side of fabric, stitching only along top curve. Clip curves, trim seam allowances, and turn. Make 8. Fuse an ABC piece to corner of D, and fuse other color palette ABC piece to other corner of D (keep 1 palette to right side and other palette to left side). Make 4. Sew D pieces together to make a square. For E, with fusible side of webbing to right side of fabric, stitch together. Clip curves, and trim allowance. Cut a small slit in webbing, and turn. Fuse to middle of square. By hand or machine, appliqué around heart and top of curves in corners using narrow blanket stitch.

HEARTS AND FLOWERS QUILT

Make 16 blocks, and sew them together in 4 rows of 4 blocks. Add narrow inside border, larger middle border, and scalloped border (see page 185). Finished size is about 44 inches square.

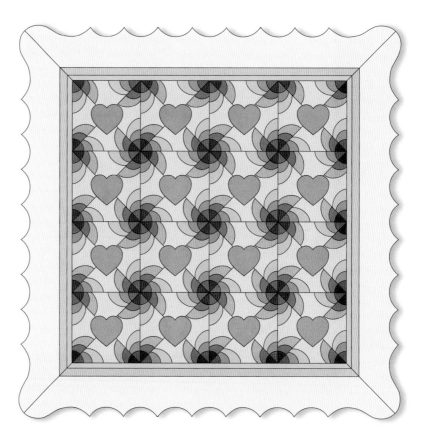

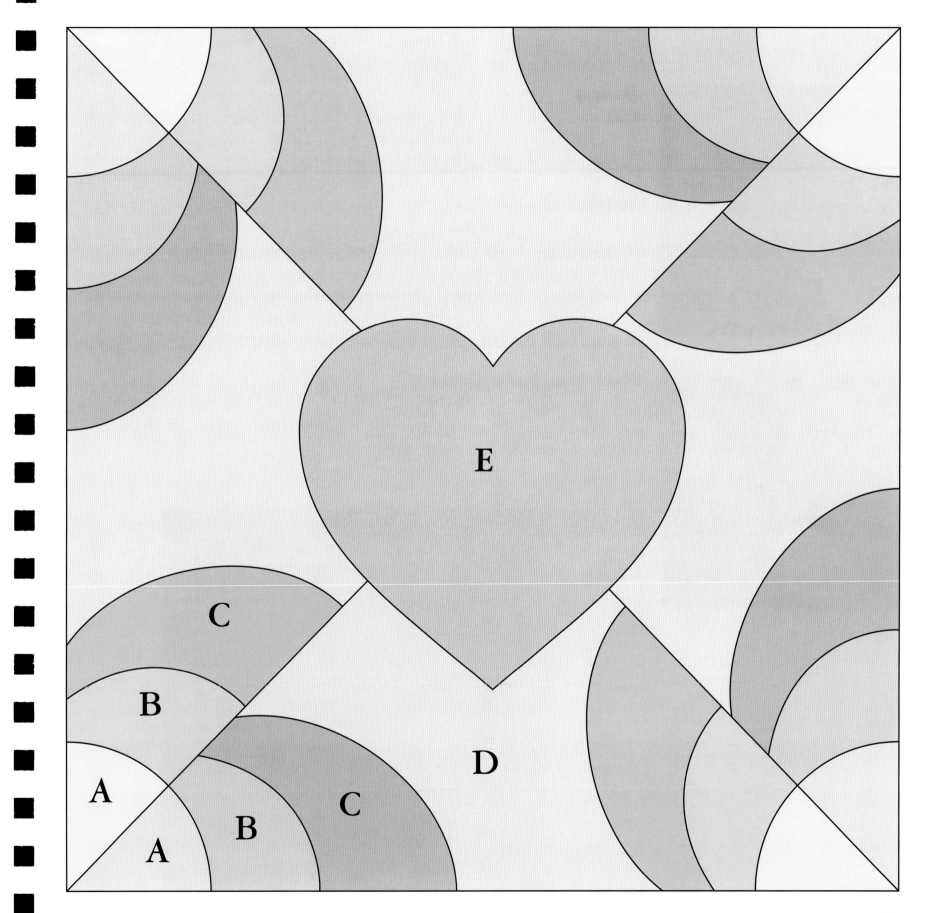

Borrow and Return

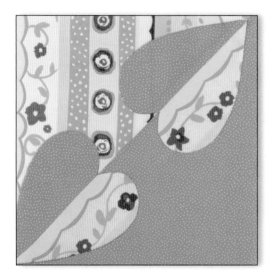

BLOCK

Cut

A: Cut 1, and cut 1 from contrasting fabric. (Pieces include area under hearts.) B: Cut 2, and cut 2 from reverse pattern and contrasting fabric.

Stitch

Stitch A to contrast A together along long sides to create a square. Stitch B and reverse B together. Make 2. On fusible webbing, trace hearts and cut out. With fusible side of webbing to right side of fabric, stitch together. Clip curves, and trim seam allowances. Cut a small slit in webbing, and turn. Make 2. Place seam of hearts on seam of square and points of hearts in corners; fuse. Heart halves should be on unlike fabrics. By hand or machine, appliqué hearts to squares using narrow blanket stitch.

GIVE AND TAKE QUILT

Make 16 blocks, and sew them together in 4 rows of 4 blocks. Add flying geese border (see page 184) and a large outer border. Appliqué hearts in corners of outer border. Finished size is about 46 inches square.

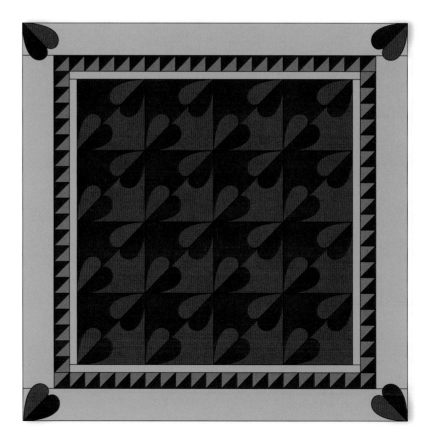

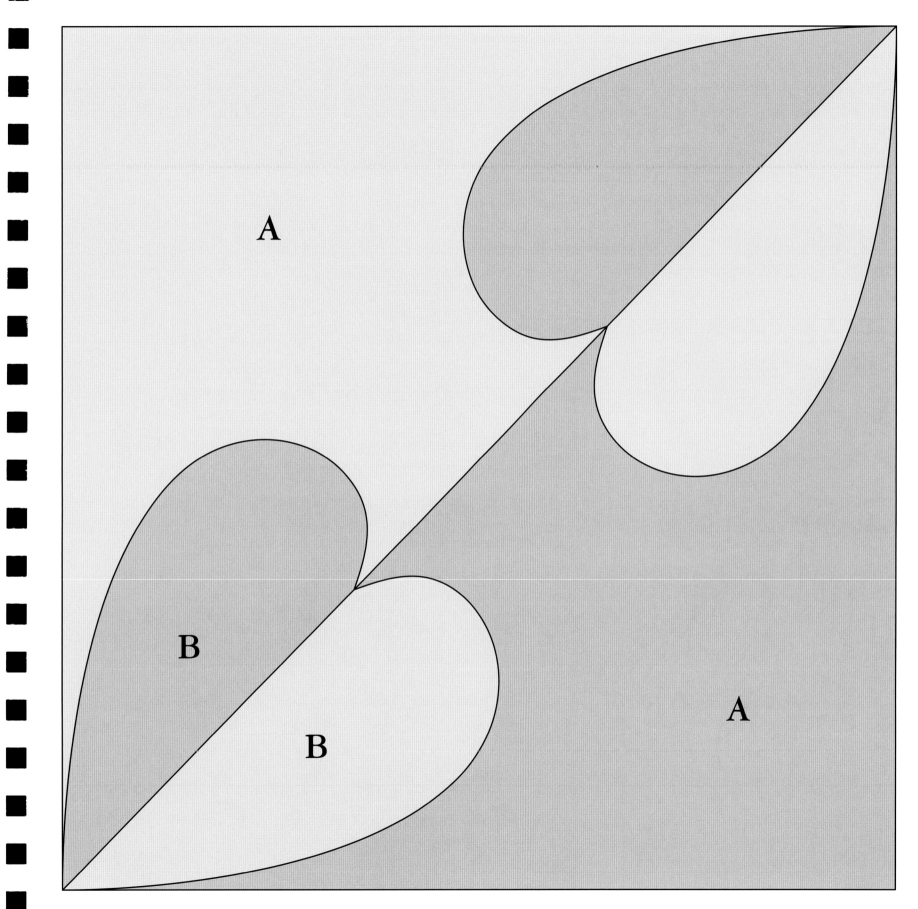

Eight-Pointed Star

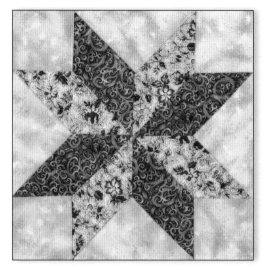

BLOCK
Cut
A: Cut 4, and cut 4 from reverse pattern and contrasting fabric. B: Cut 4. C: Cut 4.

Sew
Sew A to contrast A as shown on pattern. Make 4. Set B into V end of AA; make 4. Stitch AAB to AAB along short edge, making star half. Make 2. Sew star halves together, matching points. Set C's into sides of star to complete block.

STARRED BEAUTY QUILT
Make 16 squares, and sew them together in 4 rows of 4 blocks. Add sashing and large outer border. Finished size is about 46 inches square.

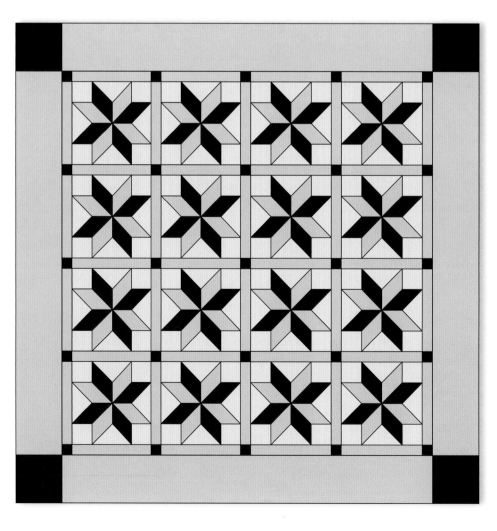

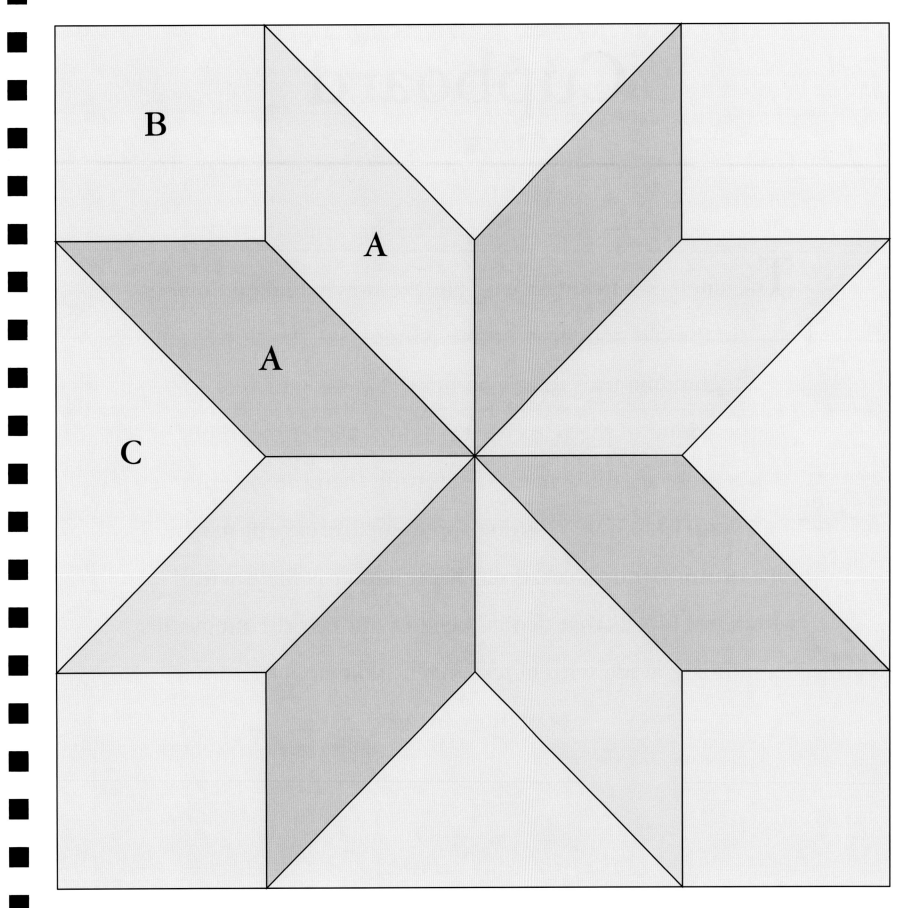

Country Cupboard

The smell of a freshly baked pie, the newly picked flowers
in the old coffeepot on the windowsill, the bowls
grandma uses to mix all her delicious goodies,
the sound of the teakettle on a cold winter morning.
Ah, is there anything more comforting than the warmth of
a country kitchen? Nothing can compare, except maybe
a country cupboard quilt! This chapter is filled with
wonderful blocks that depict some of our favorite memories
of home along with blocks that are timeless treasures
of quilting history.

Windblown Puzzle

BLOCK
Cut

A: Cut 2, and cut 2 from contrasting fabric. (Can also be 4 different fabrics.) B: Cut 4, cut 4 from contrasting fabric, and cut 4 from second contrasting fabric. C: Cut 4. D: Cut 2. E: Cut 2.

Stitch

Stitch A to contrast A; make 2. Stitch AA to AA to make a 4-patch, matching unlike fabrics. Stitch B to contrast B; make 4. Stitch BB to second contrast B, then stitch to C. Make 4. Stitch BBBC pieces to sides of 4-patch. Stitch a D to top and bottom of square. Stitch an E to each side to complete block.

BLOWIN' IN THE WIND

Make 13 blocks omitting pieces D and E. Cut 12 fabric squares same size as blocks. Stitch them together as shown. Add an inner border and an outer border using A and B pieces from block. Finished size is about 54 inches square.

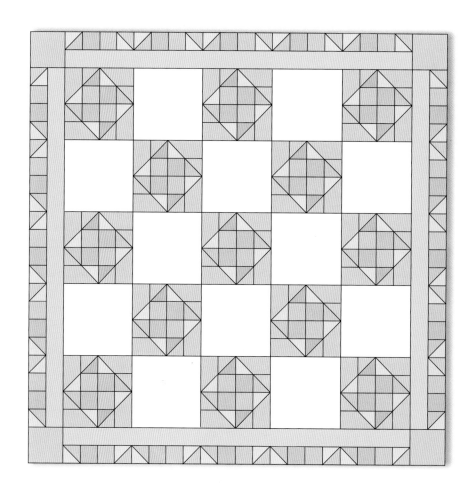

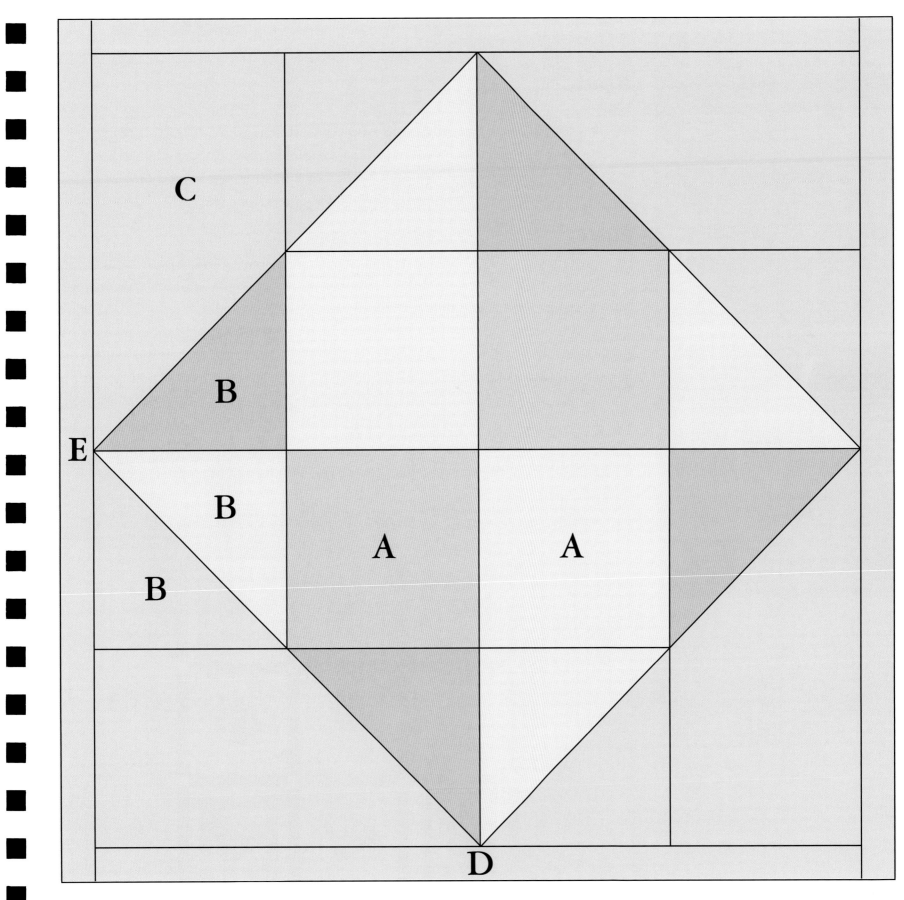

Watermelon

BLOCK
Cut

A: Cut 4, cut 20 from contrasting fabric, and cut 12 from second contrasting fabric.
B: Cut 4. C: Cut 1 (piece includes area under watermelon). Seeds: Fuse double-sided webbing to fabric, and cut 12. Watermelon pieces: Fuse double-sided webbing to fabrics, and cut 1 each. (Do not add seam allowances to fused pieces.)

Stitch

Stitch A to first contrast A; make 4. Stitch AA to B, and stitch AA to other side of B (contrast A's are next to B). Make 2. Stitch 5 contrast A's to 4 second contrast A's, alternating fabrics. Make 2. Stitch AABAA to A's strip; make 2. Stitch 3 contrast A's to 2 second contrast A's, alternating fabrics; make 2. Stitch A's strip to B; make 2. Stitch these pieces to either side of C. Stitch rows together. Fuse watermelon pieces to center, and fuse seeds to melon. By hand or machine, appliqué all fused pieces using narrow blanket stitch.

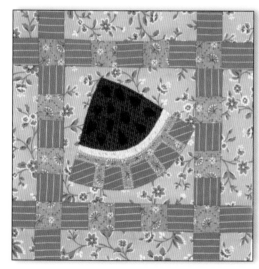

SUMMER TREATS TABLECLOTH

Make 4 blocks, and cut 5 fabric squares. Fuse a watermelon to center of each fabric square. Sew blocks and squares together, and add sashing and border. Finished size is about 40 inches square.

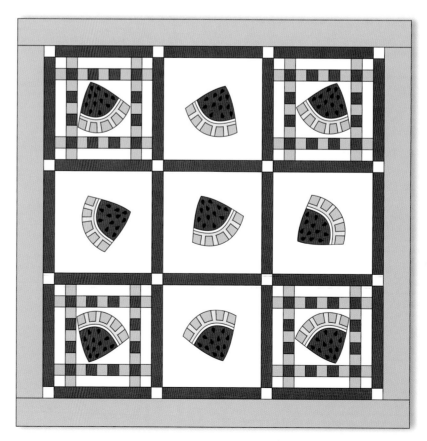

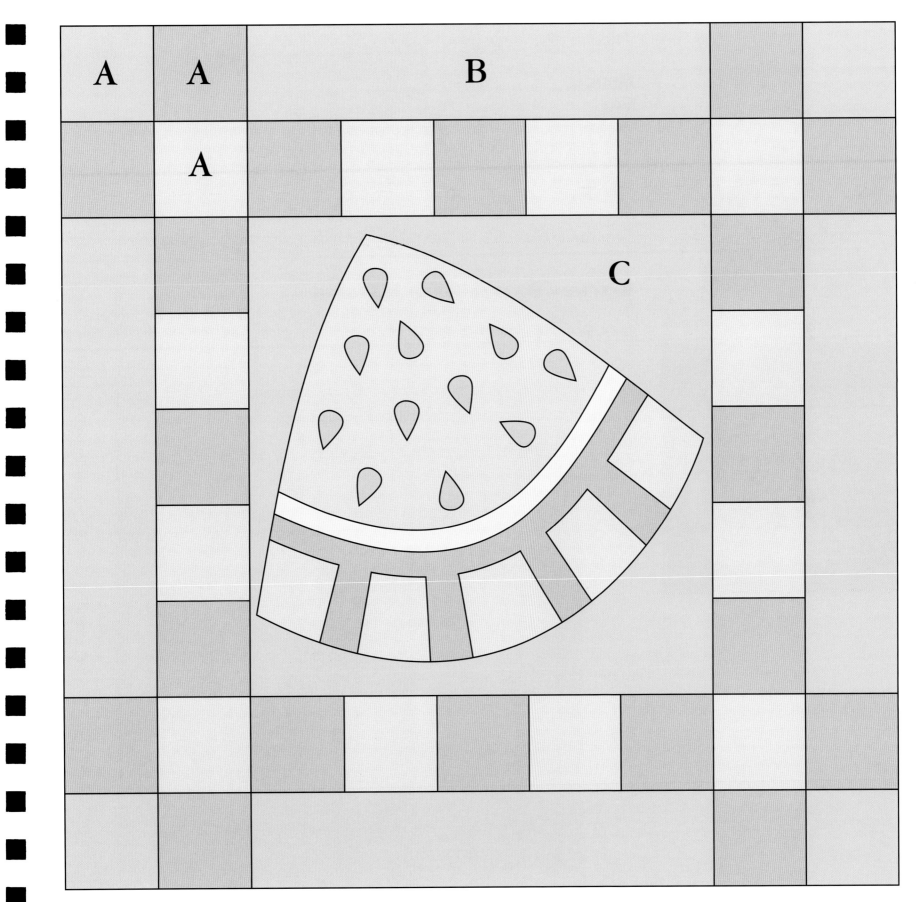

Teapot

BLOCK

Cut

Background: Cut 1. All other pieces: Fuse double-sided webbing to fabrics, and cut 1 each. (Do not add seam allowances to fused pieces.)

Stitch

Fuse pieces to background. By hand or machine, appliqué all fused pieces using narrow blanket stitch. Embroider handle using backstitch and 2 strands of floss.

KITCHEN KETTLE WALL HANGING

Make 5 blocks, and cut 5 fabric squares. Add sashing and a double border. Finished size is about 40 inches square.

Twelve Triangles

BLOCK
Cut

A: Cut 1. B: Cut 4. C: Cut 4, and cut 4 from contrasting fabric. D: Cut 4.

Stitch

Stitch a B to each side of A (middle square). Stitch C to contrast C; make 4. Stitch a CC to each side of D, matching unlike fabrics. Make 2. Stitch D to middle square, and then stitch another D to other side of middle square. Stitch rows together to complete block.

TRIANGLES PLACE MAT

Make 1 block. Stitch side borders, then add eight-pointed star border (see page 194) to top and bottom. Finished size is about 18×15 inches.

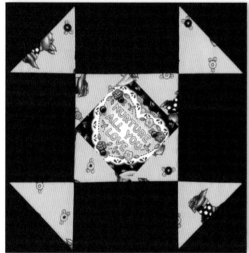

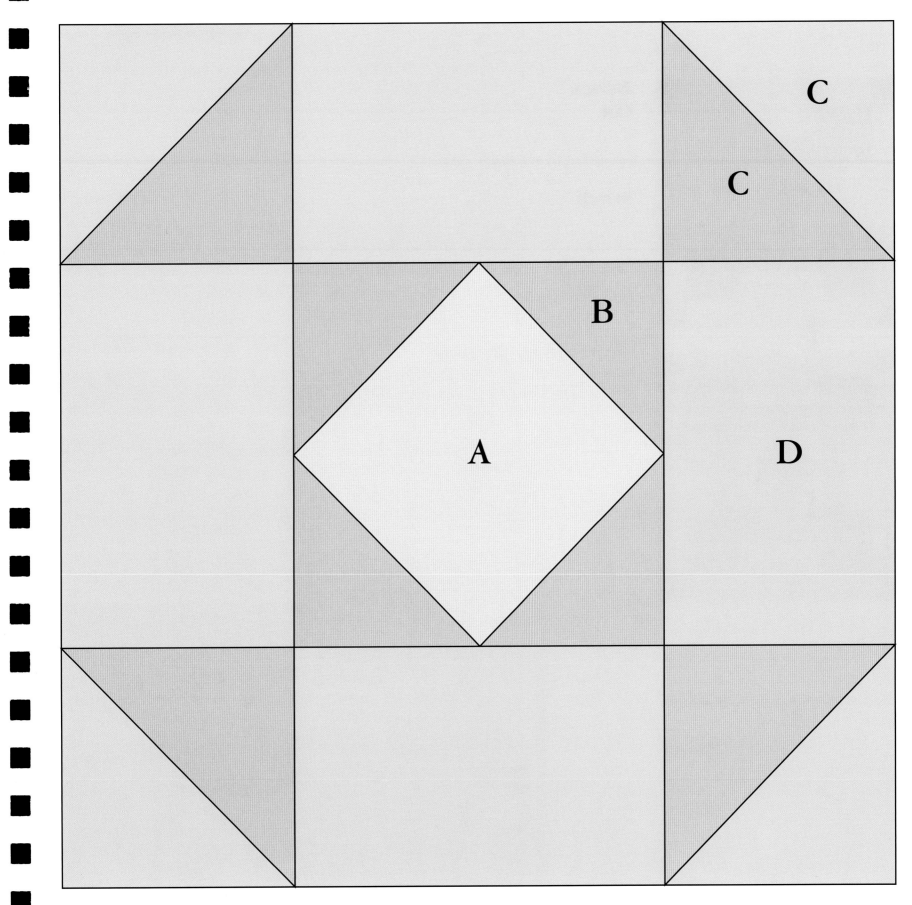

Handweave

BLOCK

Cut

A: Cut 2, and cut 2 from contrasting fabric. B: Cut 4. C: Cut 4, and cut 4 from contrasting fabric. D: Cut 4. E: Cut 4. F: Cut 4.

Stitch

Stitch A to contrast A; make 2. Stitch AA to AA, matching unlike fabrics (4-patch). Stitch a B to each side of 4-patch. Stitch C to contrast C; make 4. Stitch a D to each end of CC; make 2. Stitch CC to side of 4-patch, then stitch CC to other side of 4-patch. Stitch rows together. Stitch E to F, then stitch E to other side of F. Make 2. Stitch an F to each side of large square. Stitch an EFE to top and bottom of square to complete block.

HANDWOVEN BEAUTY

Make 15 blocks and 15 squares with EFE borders. (Make sure all blocks are same size.) Stitch together as shown. Add double borders. Finished size is about 49×58 inches.

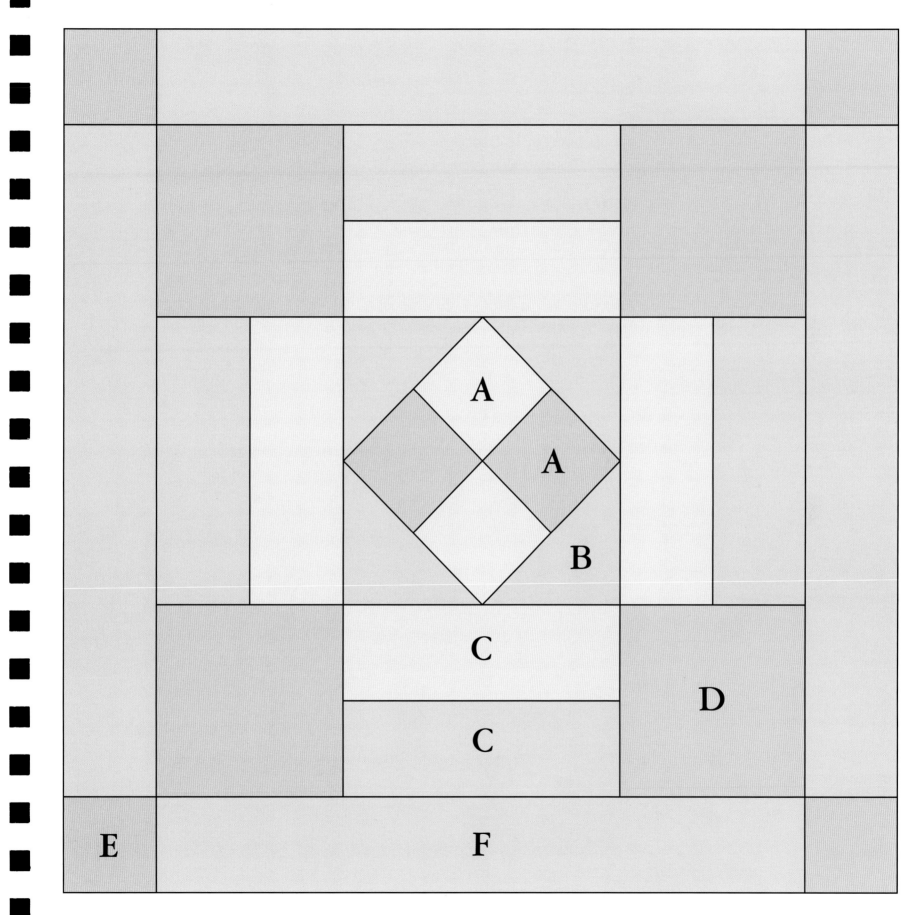

Honey Pot

BLOCK

Cut

Background: Cut 1. All other pieces: Fuse double-sided webbing to fabrics, and cut 1 each. (Do not add seam allowances to fused pieces.)

Stitch

Fuse all pieces to background square. Fuse letters to front of honey pot. By hand or machine, appliqué all fused pieces using narrow blanket stitch.

HONEY OF A WALL HANGING

Make 3 blocks, but decrease width of background square. Add sashing and an inner border. Add blocks border and outer border. Finished size is about 36×20 inches.

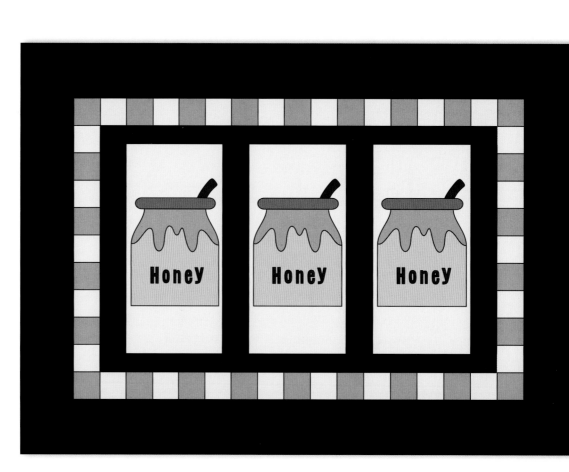

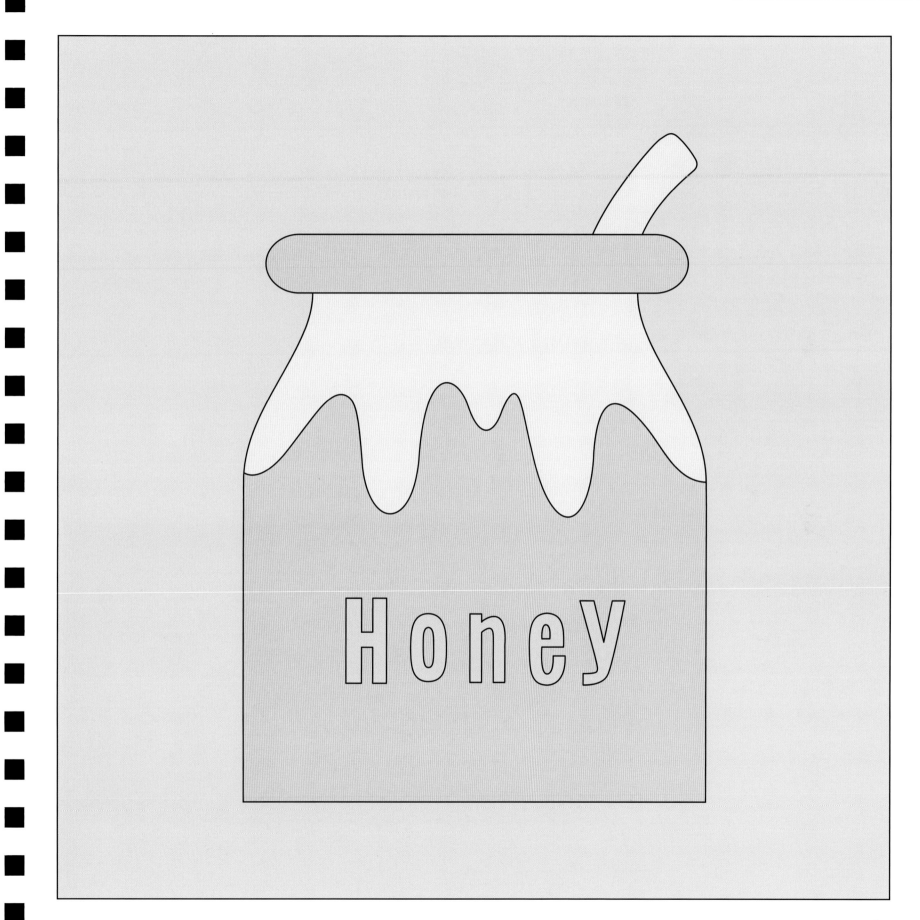

Home Sweet Home

BLOCK
Cut

Background: Cut 1. Hearts: Fuse double-sided webbing to fabric, and cut 2. Letters: Fuse double-sided webbing to fabric, and cut 1 each. Strips: Fuse double-sided webbing to fabric, and cut 4. (Do not add seam allowances to fused pieces.)

Stitch

Fuse vertical strips 1 inch in from each side. Fuse horizontal strips 1 inch in from top and bottom edges. Fuse letters and hearts in middle of square. By hand or machine, appliqué all fused pieces using narrow blanket stitch.

WELCOMING BANNER

Make 2 windblown puzzle blocks (see page 50) and 1 home sweet home block. Stitch blocks together as shown. Add inner and outer borders. Add loops for hanging. Finished size is about 35×17 inches.

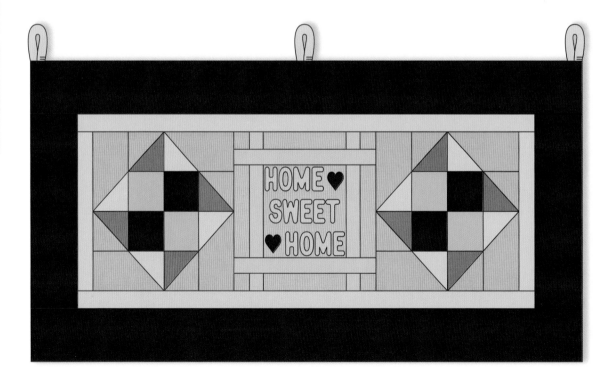

Garden of Eden

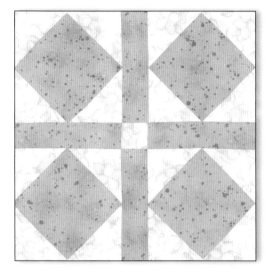

BLOCK
Cut

A: Cut 4. B: Cut 16. C: Cut 4. D: Cut 1.

Stitch

Stitch a B to each side of A (corner square). Make 4. Stitch corner square to C, then stitch another corner square to other side of C. Make 2. Stitch C to D, then stitch another C to other side of D. Stitch rows together to complete block.

PARADISE BED QUILT

Make 20 blocks, and stitch them together in 5 rows of 4 blocks. Add sashing and flowers and more border (see page 179). Finished size is about 41×51 inches.

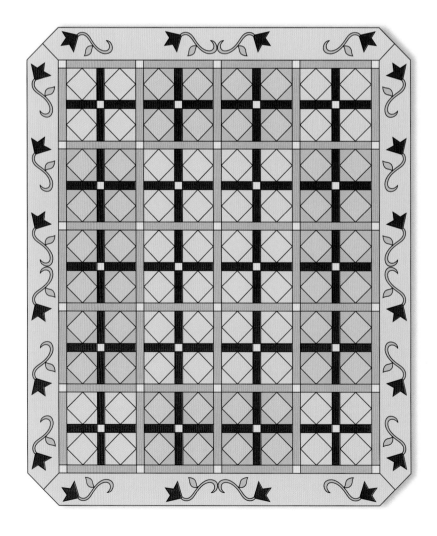

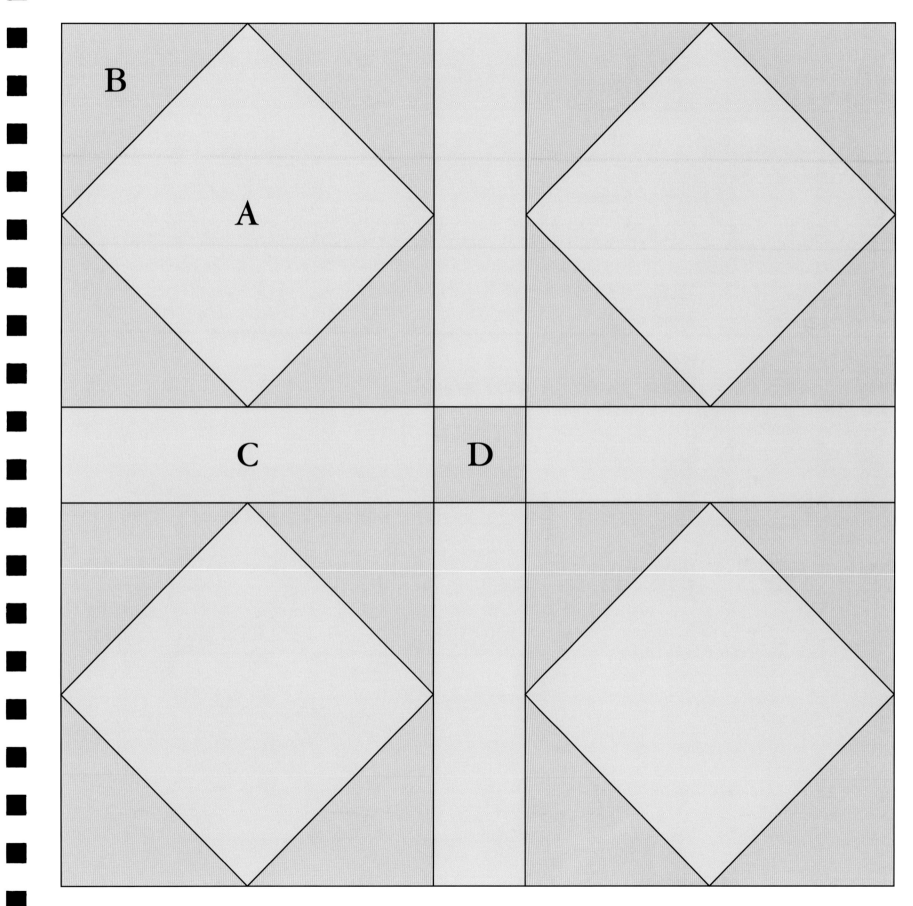

Hourglass

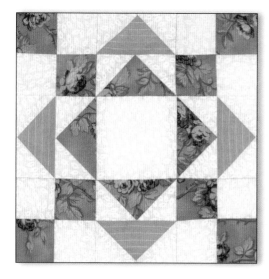

BLOCK

Cut

A: Cut 4, and cut 4 from contrasting fabric. B: Cut 16. C: Cut 8, and cut 8 from contrasting fabric. D: Cut 1.

Stitch

Stitch C to contrast C; make 8. Stitch CC to CC, matching unlike colors (4-patch). Make 4. Stitch B to A, then stitch another B to other side of A. Make 8. Stitch BAB to contrast BAB (flying geese square); make 4. Stitch 4-patch to side of flying geese square, then stitch 4-patch to other side of flying geese square. Make 2. Stitch a flying geese square to D, with points directed out. Stitch another flying geese square to other side of D, with points directed out. Stitch rows together to complete block.

TIMELESS WALL HANGING

Make 4 blocks, and stitch them together in 2 rows of 2 blocks. Add sashing and border. Finished size is about 22½ inches square.

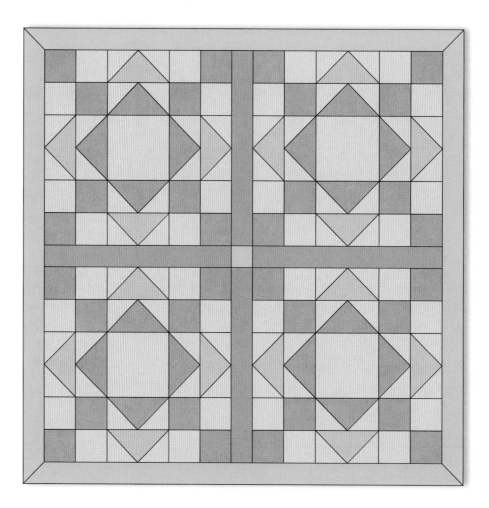

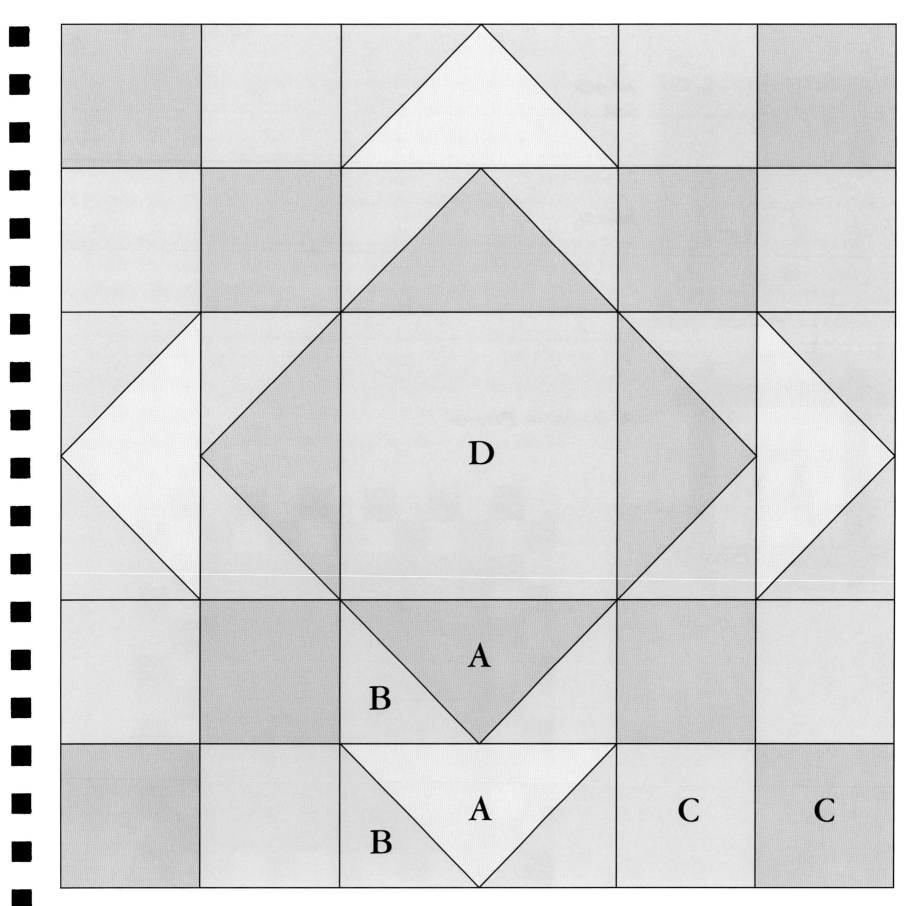

Churn Dash

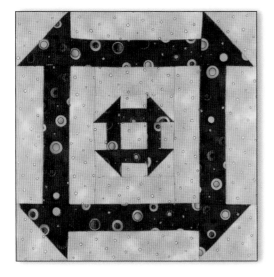

BLOCK
Cut
A: Cut 4, and cut 4 from contrasting fabric. B: Cut 4, and cut 4 from contrasting fabric. C: Cut 1. D: Cut 2. E: Cut 6, and cut 4 from contrasting fabric. F: Cut 4, and cut 4 from contrasting fabric.

Stitch
Stitch A to contrast A; make 4. Stitch B to contrast B; make 4. Stitch AA to BB, then stitch AA to other side of BB (note where contrast fabrics are placed throughout). Make 2. Stitch BB to C, then stitch BB to other side of C. Sew rows together to make center square. Stitch a D to top and bottom of center square. Stitch an E to each side of center square. Stitch E to contrast E; make 4. Stitch F to contrast F; make 4. Stitch FF to EE, then stitch FF to other side of EE. Make 2. Stitch an EE to each side of center square. Stitch rows together to complete block.

A DASHING PILLOW
Make 1 block. Add a double border of squares. Finished size is about 17 inches square.

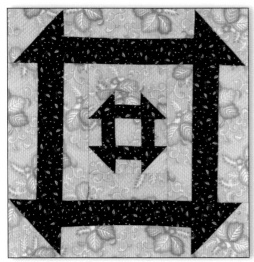

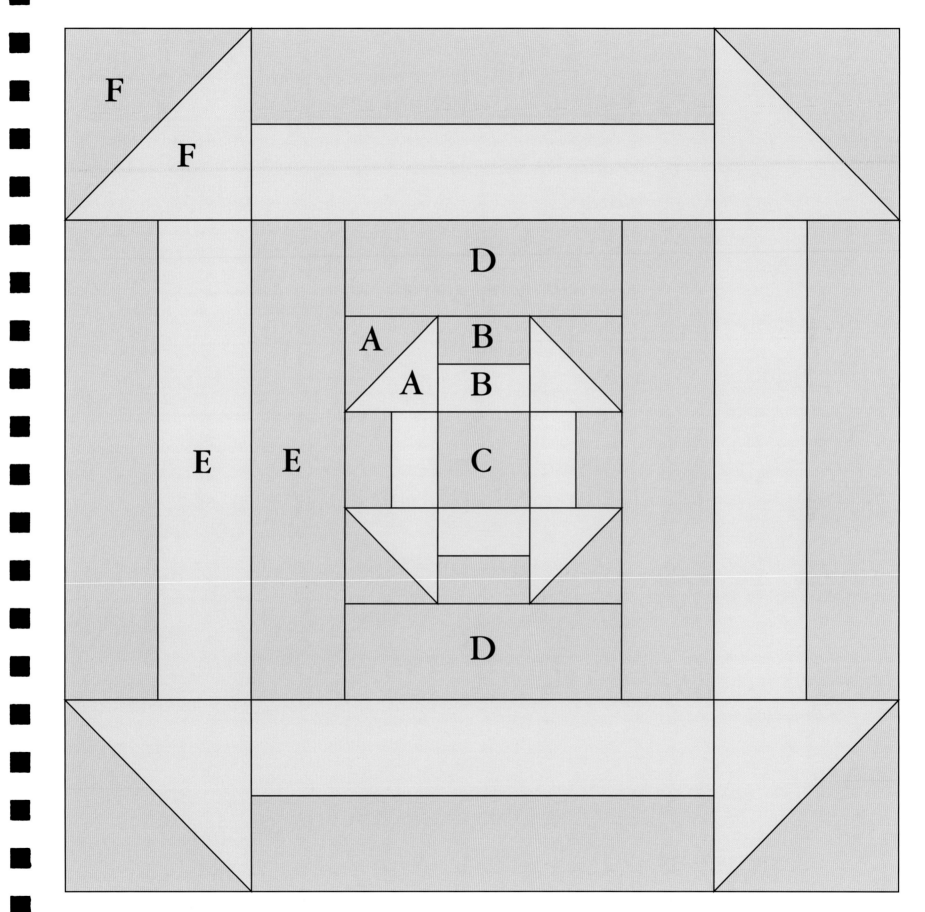

Rooster

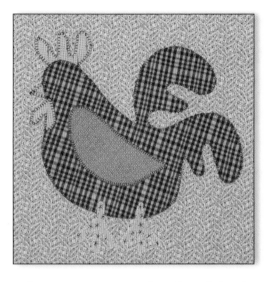

BLOCK
Cut
Background: Cut 1. All appliqué pieces: Fuse double-sided webbing to fabrics, then cut out. Feet: Cut 2. All other pieces: Cut 1. (Do not add seam allowances to fused pieces.)

Stitch
Fuse rooster body to background square. Fuse beak, comb, wattle, wing, and feet to rooster. By hand or machine, appliqué all fused pieces using narrow blanket stitch.

COCK-A-DOODLE TABLE RUNNER
Make 9 blocks, and cut 9 fabric squares. Sew together as shown. Add blocks for side borders. Finished size is about 60×27 inches.

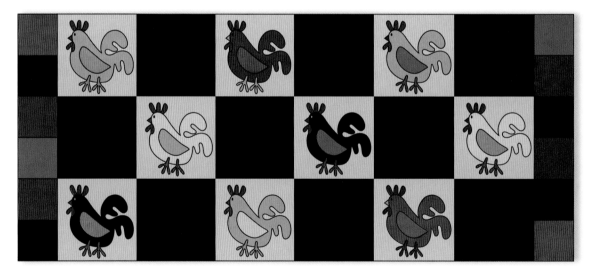

Heart Can

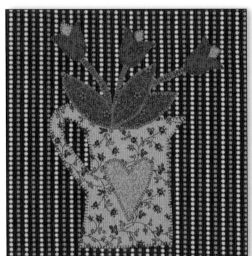

BLOCK

Cut

Background: Cut 1. All other pieces: Fuse double-sided webbing to fabrics. Flowers and flower centers: Cut 3 each. All other pieces: Cut 1 each. (Do not add seam allowances to fused pieces.)

Stitch

Fuse watering can, leaves, stems, and flowers to background square. Fuse heart to can. By hand or machine, appliqué all fused pieces using narrow blanket stitch.

HEARTS AND FLOWERS

Make 5 blocks, and cut 4 fabric squares. Cut 4 hearts, and fuse webbing to fabric. Fuse hearts to fabric squares. Sew together as shown. Add inner and outer borders. Finished size is about 36 inches square.

Double Heart

BLOCK

Cut

A: Cut 2. B: Cut 2. C: Cut 1. D: Cut 2. E: Cut 2. F: Cut 1, and cut 1 from reverse pattern (pieces include area under appliqué). G: Cut 1. H: Cut 1 (piece includes area under appliqué). I: Cut 2. J: Cut 1, and cut 1 from reverse pattern. K: Cut 2 (pieces include area under appliqué). L: Cut 1. Small heart: Fuse double-sided webbing to fabric, and cut 1 (do not add seam allowance).

Stitch

Row 1: Stitch A to B; stitch C to other side of B. Stitch B to other side of C, and stitch A to other side of B. *Row 2:* Stitch E to left top of F; stitch G to right side of EF; stitch reverse F to G. Stitch E to top right of F. Stitch H to bottom, and stitch a D to each side. *Row 3:* Stitch I to J, then stitch on K. Make 2 (1 is reverse pattern). Stitch squares together. Sew rows together in order. Stitch L to top. Fuse heart to middle of square. By hand or machine, appliqué heart using narrow blanket stitch.

HEARTS IN A ROW WALL HANGING

Make 5 blocks, and stitch them together in a row. Add border and bows. Finished size is about 49×13 inches.

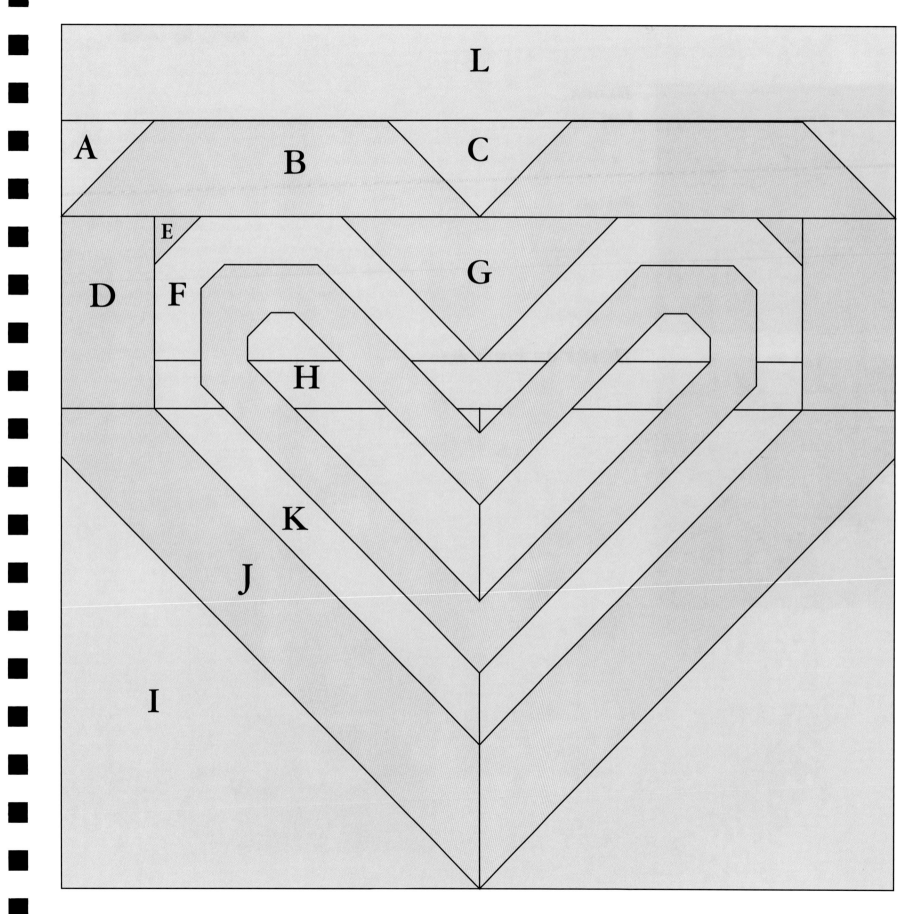

Attic Window

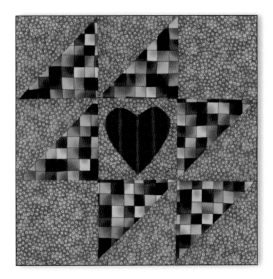

BLOCK
Cut

A: Cut 6, and cut 6 from contrasting fabric. B: Cut 3. Heart: Fuse double-sided webbing to fabric, and cut 1 (do not add seam allowance).

Stitch

Sew A to contrast A; make 6. Stitch AA to AA, matching unlike fabrics, then stitch on B. Make 2. Stitch AA to B, with contrast triangle at bottom, then stitch on AA, with contrast triangle at top. Stitch rows together, with the bottom row sewn on starting with B square. Fuse heart to center square. By hand or machine, appliqué heart using narrow blanket stitch.

HEART ON YOUR BAG

Make 1 block, and construct bag with drawstring. Finished size depends on size of bag.

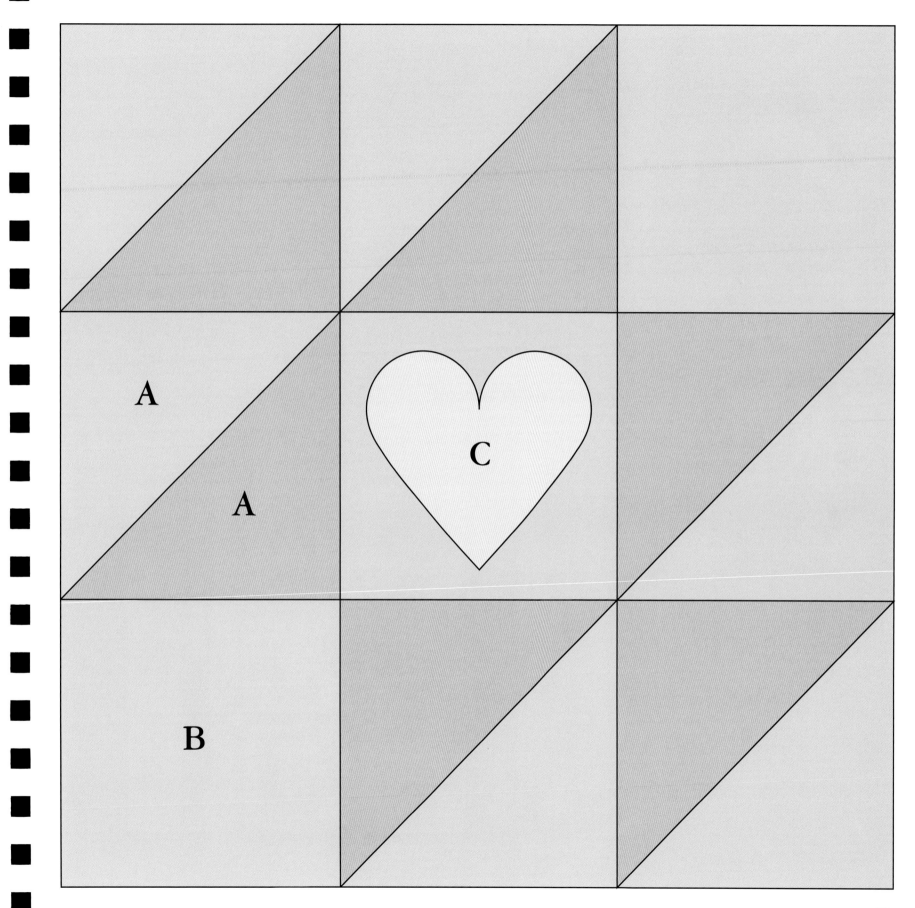

Cherry Basket

BLOCK

Cut

A: Cut 1. B: Cut 1, and cut 1 from reverse pattern. C: Cut 1. D: Cut 1, and cut 1 from reverse pattern. E: Cut 1 (piece includes area under appliqués). F: Cut 1 (piece includes area under appliqué). All appliqué pieces: Fuse double-sided webbing to fabrics before cutting out. Cherry 1: Cut 4. Cherry 2: Cut 2. Leaves: Cut 3 (use front leaf for pattern). Stems: Cut 2. Handle: Cut 1. (Do not add seam allowances to fused pieces.)

Stitch

Stitch B to C, and stitch reverse B to other side of C. Stitch D to E, and stitch reverse D to other side of E. Stitch BCB to A; stitch DED to top of BCBA. Stitch F to top of DEDBCBA. Place and fuse stems, cherries, leaves, and handle in place. By hand or machine, appliqué all fused pieces using narrow blanket stitch.

BOUNTY OF BASKETS

Make 9 blocks, and stitch them together in 3 rows of 3 blocks. Add sashing and inner and outer borders. Finished size is about 38 inches square.

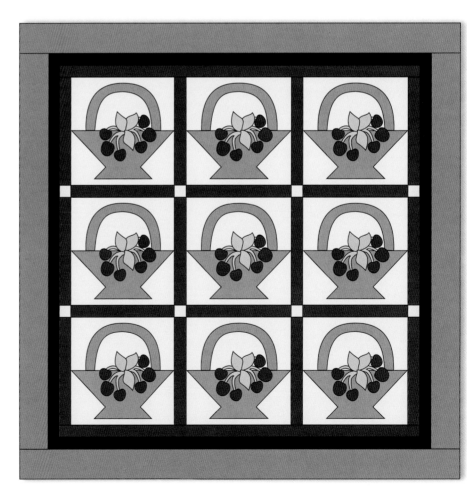

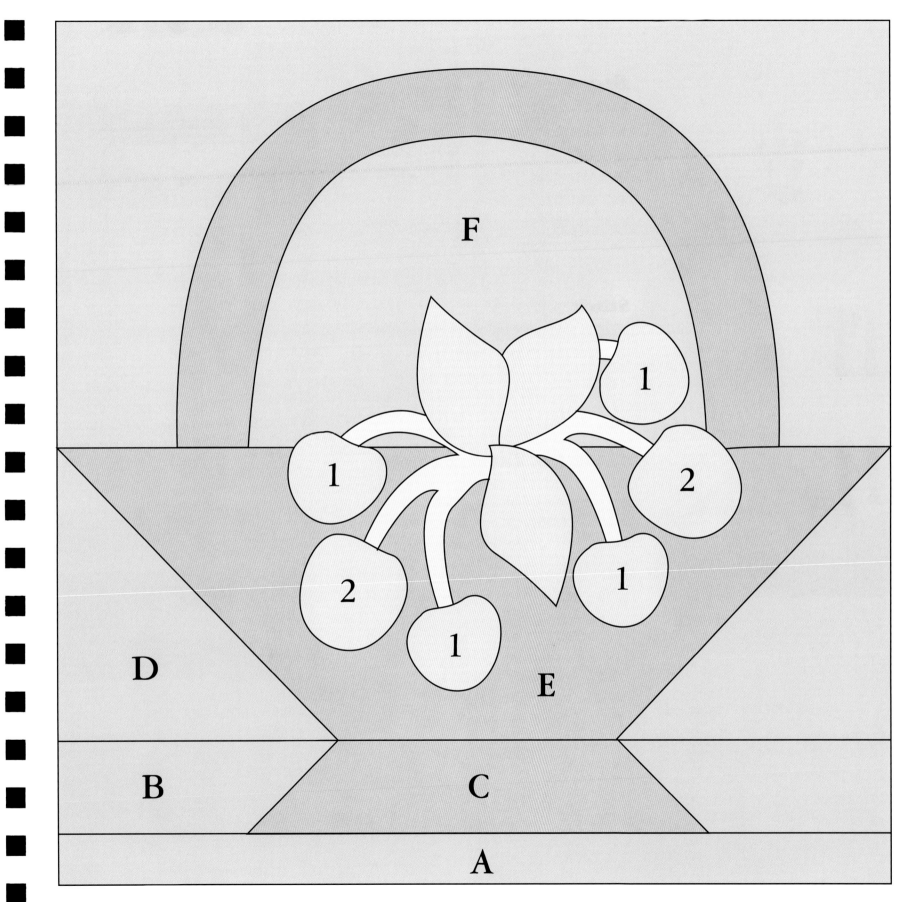

Apple Pie

BLOCK
Cut

A: Cut 1 (piece includes area under appliqué). B: Cut 1 (piece includes area under appliqué). Hearts: Fuse double-sided webbing to fabric, and cut 3. Other pieces: Fuse double-sided webbing to fabrics, and cut 1. (Do not add seam allowances to fused pieces.)

Stitch

Stitch A to B. Fuse pieces to AB; fuse hearts to top of pie. By hand or machine, appliqué all fused pieces using narrow blanket stitch. Embroider steam using backstitch and 2 strands of floss.

CUTIE PIE TABLE RUNNER
Using a shorter background piece, make 2 blocks. Stitch blocks to either side of a length of fabric. Quilt hearts on fabric. Finished size depends on length of fabric.

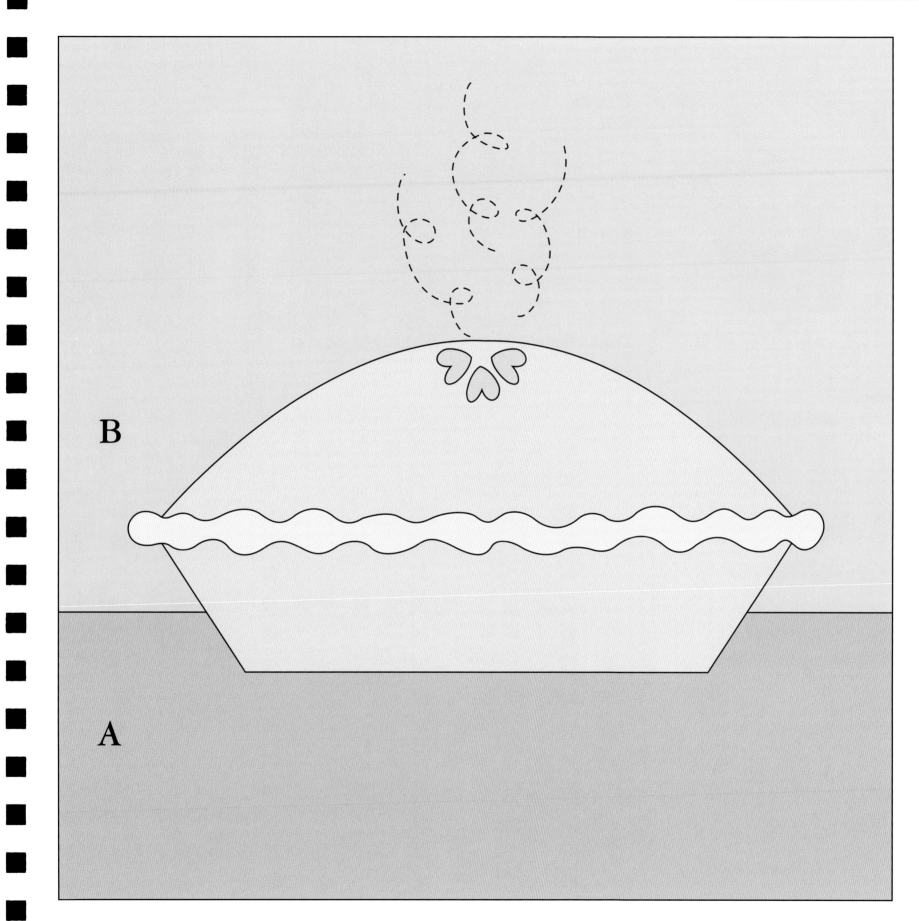

B

A

Grandma's Bowls

BLOCK

Cut

Background: Cut 1. All appliqué pieces: Fuse double-sided webbing to fabrics, then cut out. Dots on bottom bowl: Cut 10 or 11. All other pieces: Cut 1 each. (Do not add seam allowances to fused pieces.)

Stitch

Fuse pieces to background square. By hand or machine, appliqué all fused pieces using narrow blanket stitch. Make French knots in stripe of top bowl using 2 strands of embroidery floss (marked by X's on pattern).

GRANDMA'S BOWLS WALL HANGING

Make 9 blocks: Make 3 blocks with all bowls and 6 blocks with only 1 or 2 bowls. Stitch blocks together in 3 rows of 3 blocks. Add block strips as sashing and blocks border. Finished size is about 35 inches square.

City Streets

BLOCK

Cut

A: Cut 8, and cut 8 from contrasting fabric. B–I: Cut 4 each.

Stitch

Stitch A to contrast A; make 2. Stitch AA to AA, matching unlike fabrics (4-patch). Stitch 4-patch to B, then stitch on C. Continue adding strips, D, then E; F, then G; H, then I, as shown on pattern. Make 4 squares, and sew them together with 4-patches in outer corners.

AVENUES OF DELIGHT QUILT

Make 30 blocks, and stitch them together in 6 rows of 5 blocks. Add border. Finished size is about 49×58 inches.

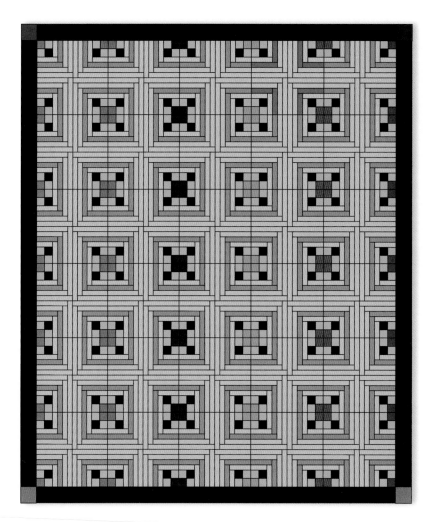

84

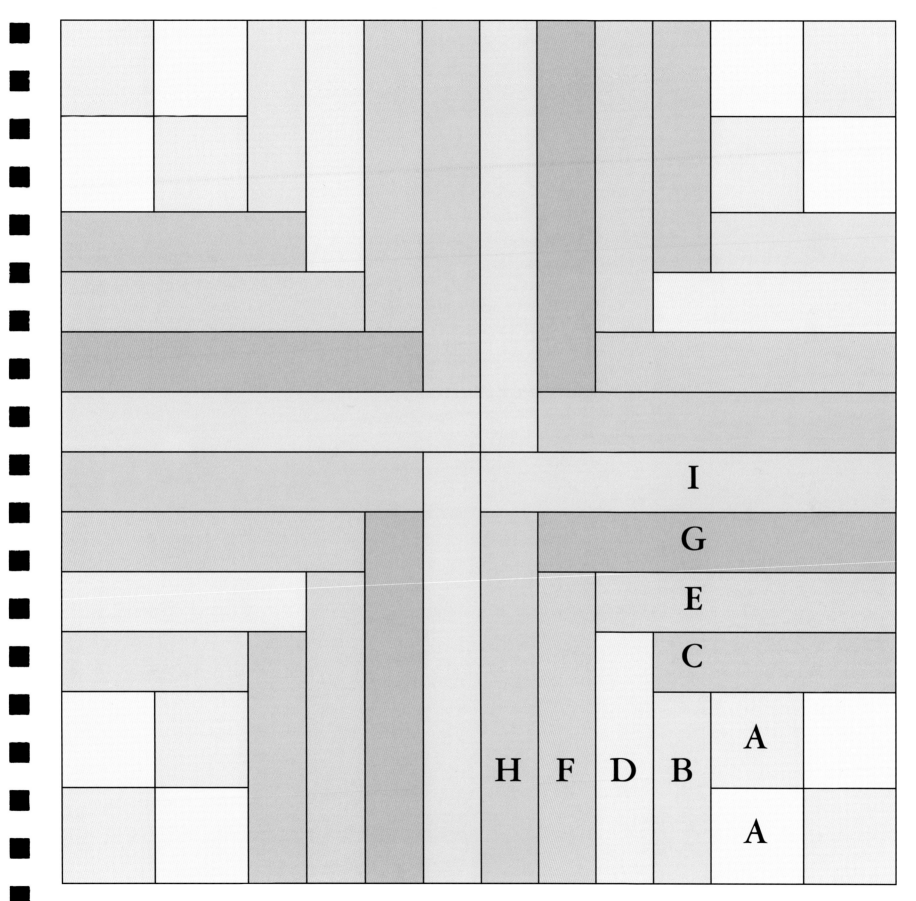

Chimneys and Cornerstones

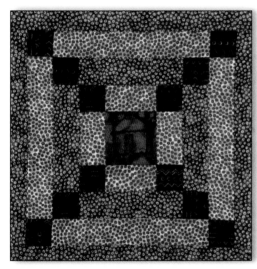

BLOCK

Cut

A: Cut 1. B: Cut 12. C: Cut 4. D: Cut 4. E: Cut 4. F: Cut 2. G: Cut 2.

Stitch

Stitch B to C, and stitch B to other side of C. Make 2. Stitch C to A, then stitch C to other side of A. Stitch BCB to CAC, then stitch another BCB to block to form center square. Stitch B to D, then stitch B to other side of D. Make 2. Stitch D to side of center square, and then stitch D to other side of square. Sew a BDB to top and bottom of center square. Stitch B to E, then stitch B to other side of E. Make 2. Stitch E to side of center square, and then stitch E to other side of square. Sew a BEB to top and bottom of square. Stitch an F to top and bottom of square. Stitch a G to each side to complete block.

CHIMNEY POT HOLDER

Make 1 block, and use very thick padding. Add a loop for hanging. Finished size is about 9 inches square.

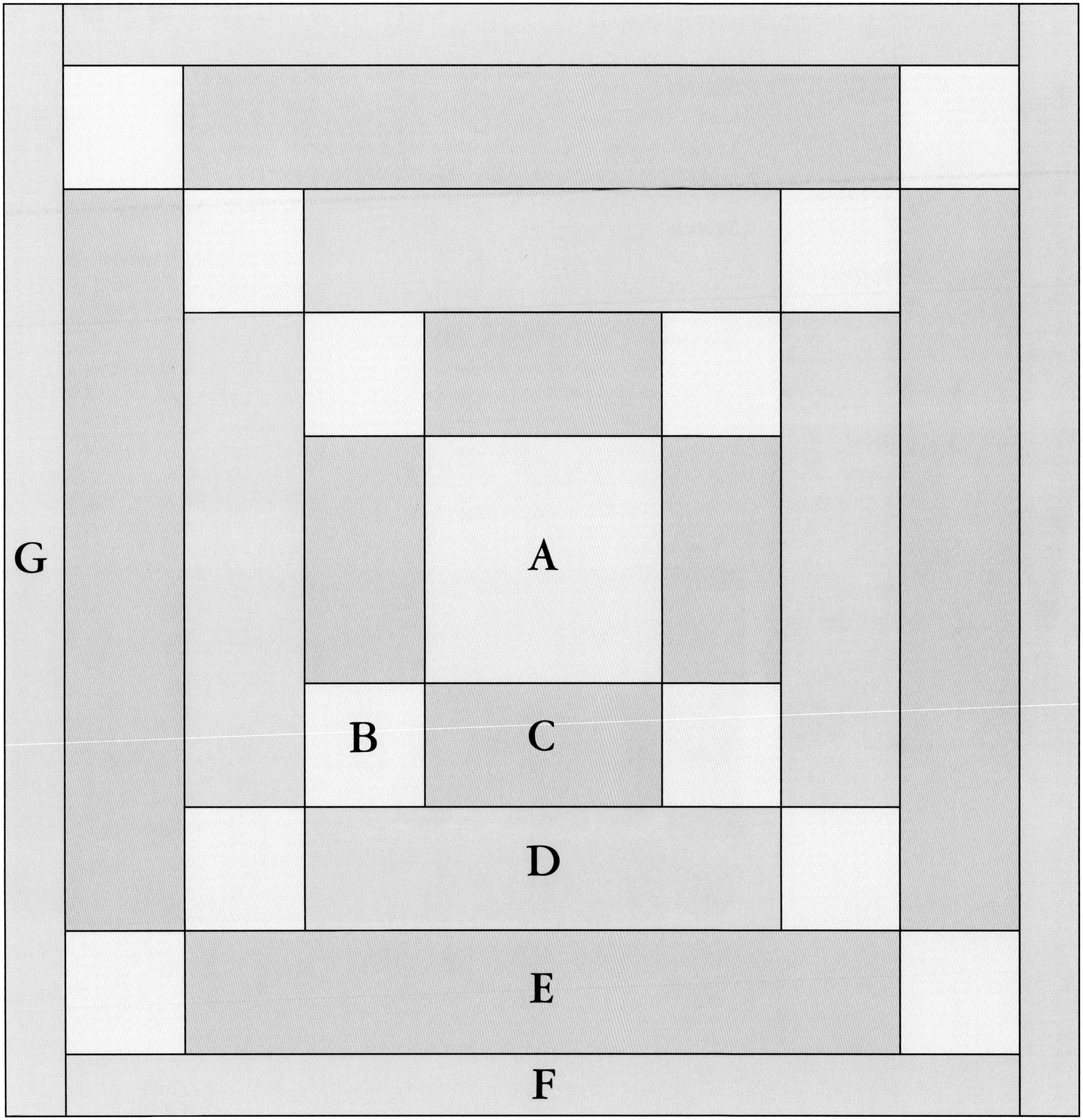
G
A
B
C
D
E
F

Apple Cider

BLOCK

Cut

Background: Cut 1. All other pieces: Fuse double-sided webbing to fabrics, and cut 1 each. (Do not add seam allowances to fused pieces.)

Stitch

Fuse pieces to background square. Fuse label to bottle and letters to label. By hand or machine, appliqué all fused pieces using narrow blanket stitch.

SIPPING CIDER WALL HANGING

Make 3 blocks, and cut out 4 more complete apples. Stitch blocks together in a row. Add sashing and border. Fuse apples to corner squares. Finished size is about 35×15 inches.

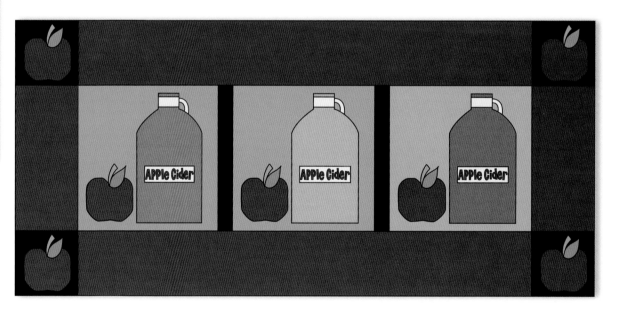

Traditional Treasures

■◆●◆■

Quilts remind us of cold winter nights and a blazing

fireplace, the warmth and comfort of a grandma's hug,

and even the amazing bravery of the pioneers who settled

much of North America. This chapter is filled

with quilt blocks that are timeless treasures—blocks

that have been stitched with love for hundreds of years.

While new fabrics can give historical blocks a modern twist,

they will still retain their old-time, special appeal.

So look through this chapter, and you'll soon find

something to make your stitching fingers

itching to get started!

Traditional Fan

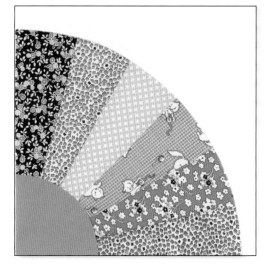

BLOCK

Cut

A: Cut 1. B: Cut 6 (from different fabrics). C: Cut 1.

Stitch

Sew B to B. Make 3. Sew BB to BB, then stitch to last BB. Stitch A to inside edge of B's. Stitch C to outside edge of B's.

FANFARE MANTEL RUNNER

Make number of blocks needed. Place squares on point, and stitch triangles between squares. Size depends on length needed for mantel.

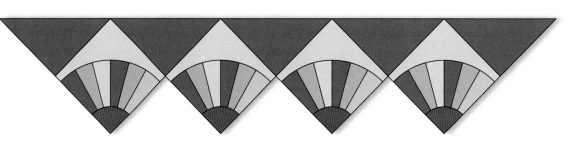

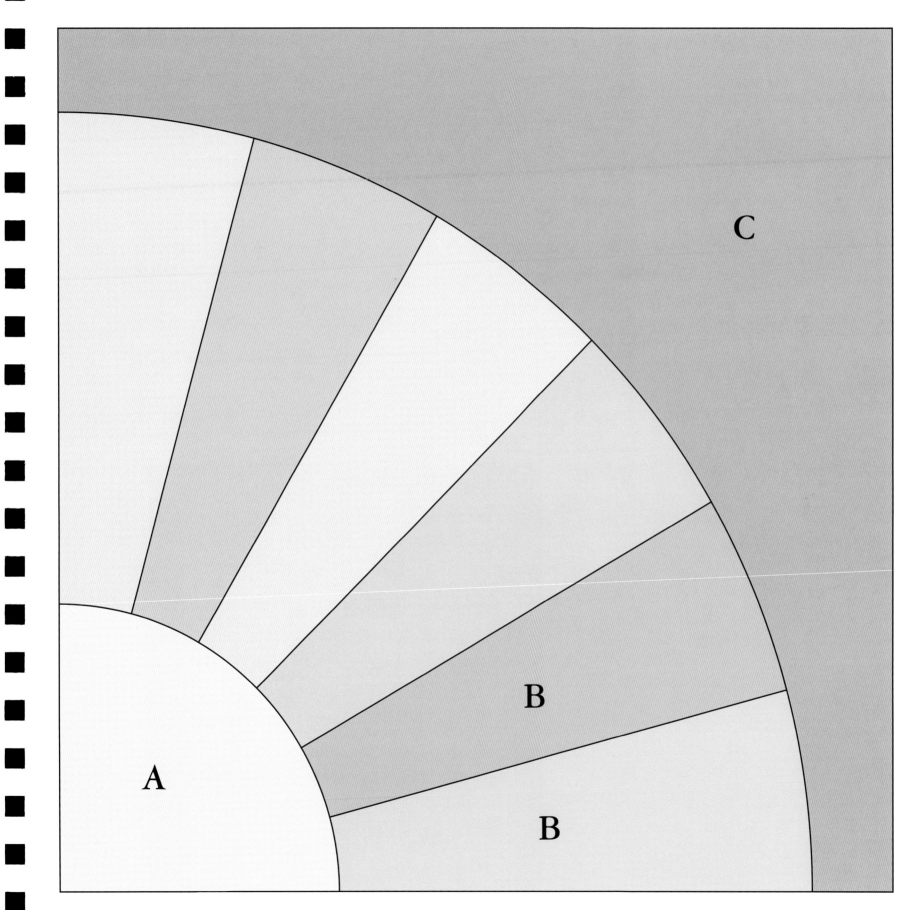

Stained Glass

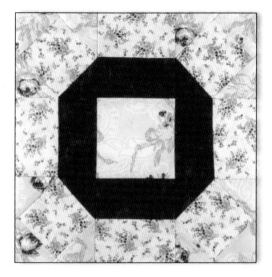

BLOCK

Cut

A: Cut 4. B: Cut 12, and cut 4 from contrasting fabric. C: Cut 4, and cut 4 from contrasting fabric. D: Cut 1.

Stitch

To make corner square, stitch a B to each side of A (add only 1 contrast B to each A). Make 4. Stitch C to contrast C; make 4. Stitch a corner square to each side of CC, matching fabrics. Make 2. Stitch CC to D, and stitch CC to other side of D. Stitch rows together to complete block.

WINDOW PANE QUILT

Make 42 blocks, and stitch them together in 7 rows of 6 blocks. Add sashing and stop sign border (see page 186). Finished size is about 60×69 inches.

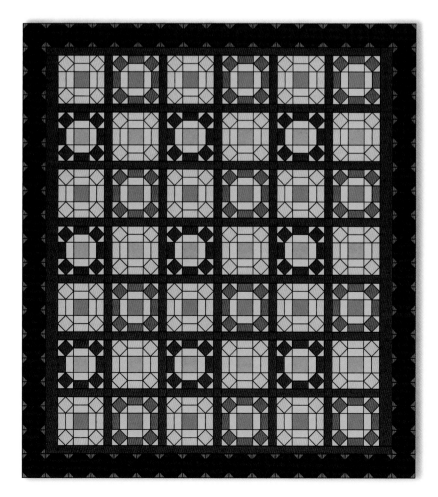

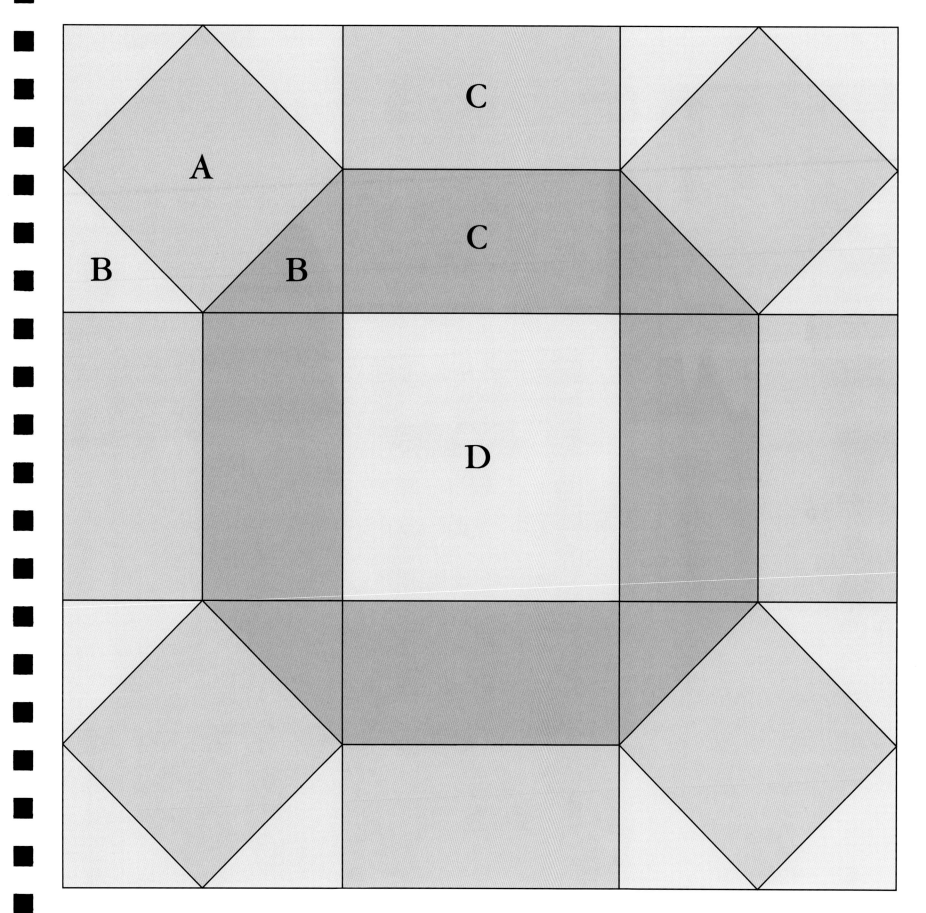

Square upon Square

BLOCK
Cut

A: Cut 1. B: Cut 4. C: Cut 4. D: Cut 4. E: Cut 4.

Stitch

Sew B's to sides of A. Stitch C's to sides of AB. Stitch D's to sides of ABC. Stitch E's to sides of ABCD. Make sure piece is square after each step.

COMFY QUILTED BED LINENS

Stitch blocks along top of comforter and sides of pillowcases. Add borders. Finished size depends on size of comforter and pillowcases.

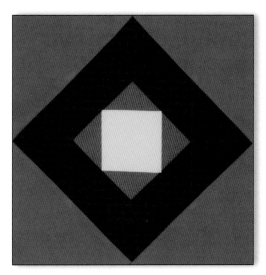

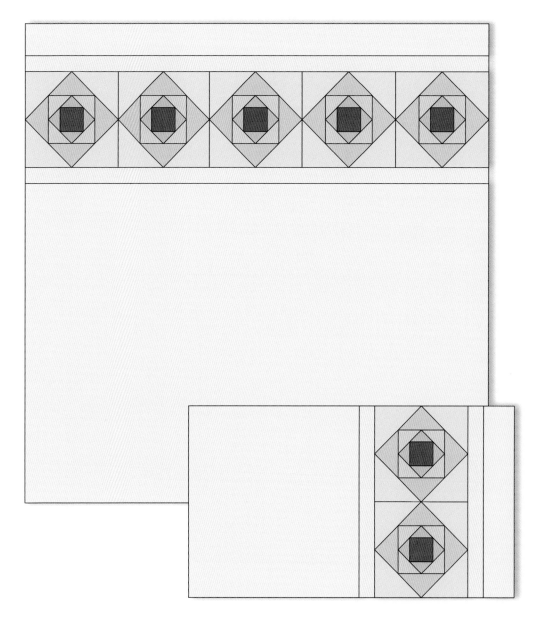

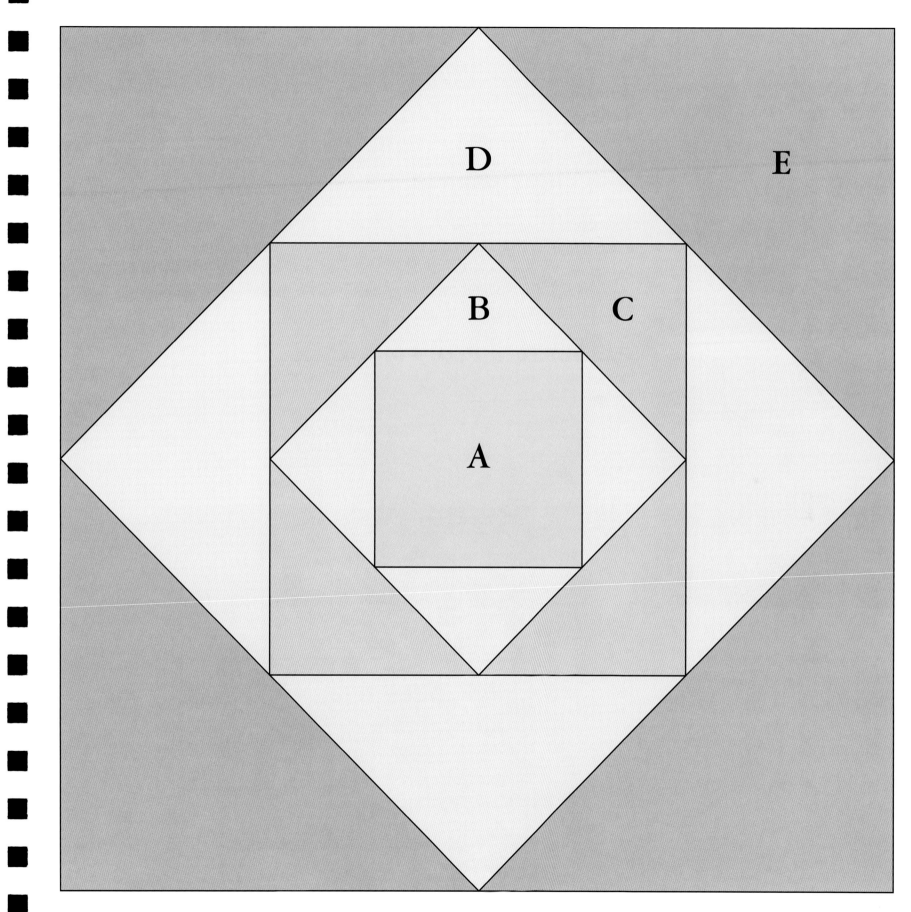

Palm Tree

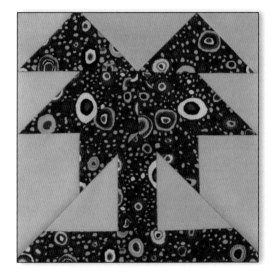

BLOCK
Cut
A: Cut 4. B: Cut 2, and cut 1 from background fabric. C: Cut 2, and cut 2 from reverse pattern. (Variation: Cut 2 C's from contrast fabric.) D: Cut 1, and cut 1 from reverse pattern. E: Cut 2. F: Cut 1. G: Cut 1.

Stitch
Stitch A to B; stitch background B to other side of B. Stitch B to other side of background B, and stitch A to end. Stitch C to reverse C; make 2. Stitch A to CC, then stitch on D; make 2. Stitch E to F, then stitch E to other side of F. Stitch G to bottom of EFE. Stitch pieces together to complete block.

PROTECT YOUR PALM POT HOLDER
Make 1 block, and pad it well. Add border and loop for hanging. Finished size is about 12 inches square.

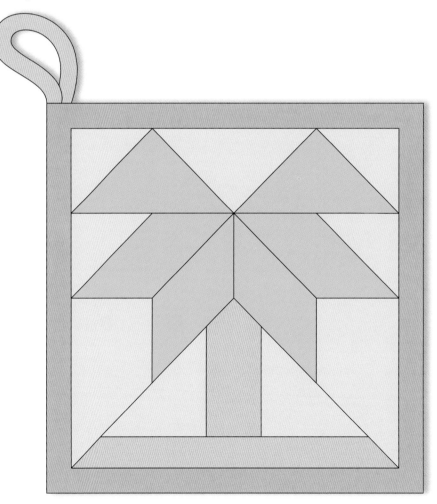

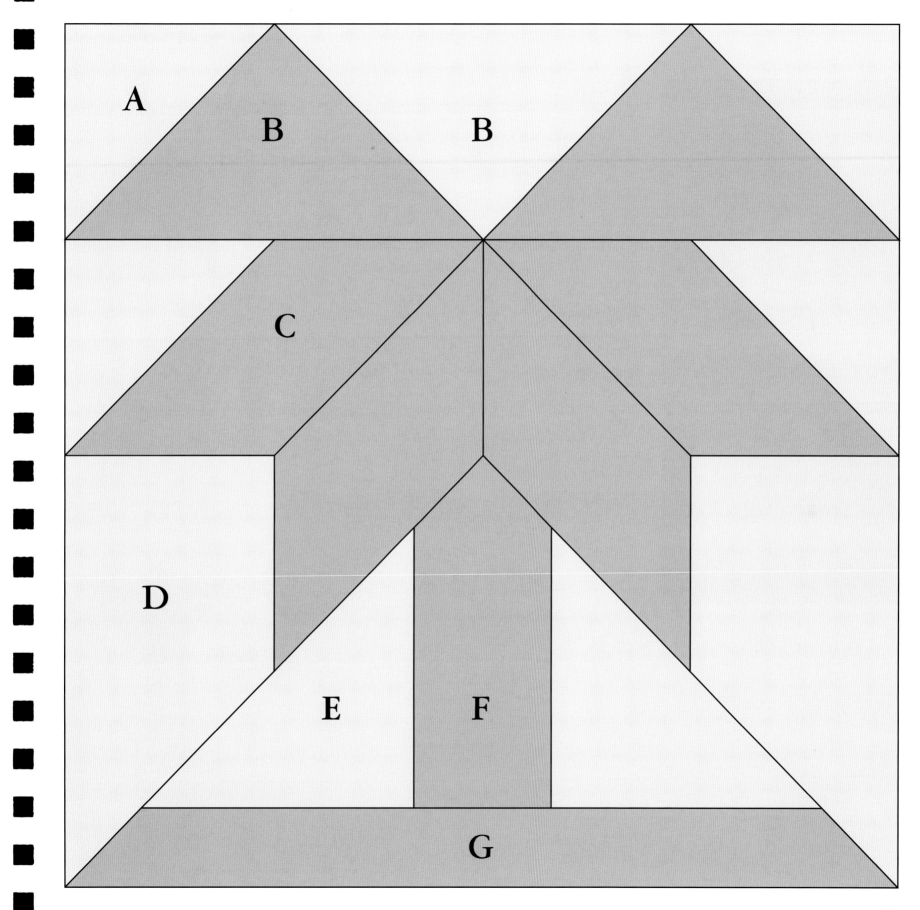

Ohio Star

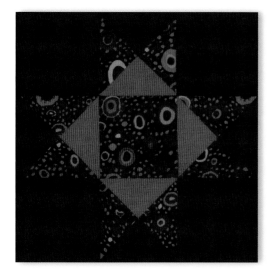

BLOCK
Cut

A: Cut 8, and cut 8 from background fabric. B: Cut 1, and cut 4 from background fabric.

Stitch

Stitch A to background A; make 8. Stitch AA to AA, matching unlike fabrics. Make 4. Stitch background B to AAAA, and then stitch background B to other side of AAAA, matching unlike fabrics. Make 2. Stitch AAAA to B, and then stitch AAAA to other side of B. Stitch rows together to complete block.

STARRY TABLE RUNNER

Make 4 blocks. Stitch blocks together in a row, adding 2-inch sashing. Add side borders and triangles at ends. Sew tassels at points of triangles. Finished size is about 59×13 inches.

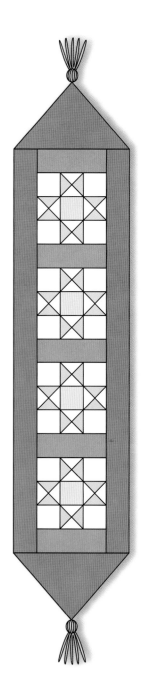

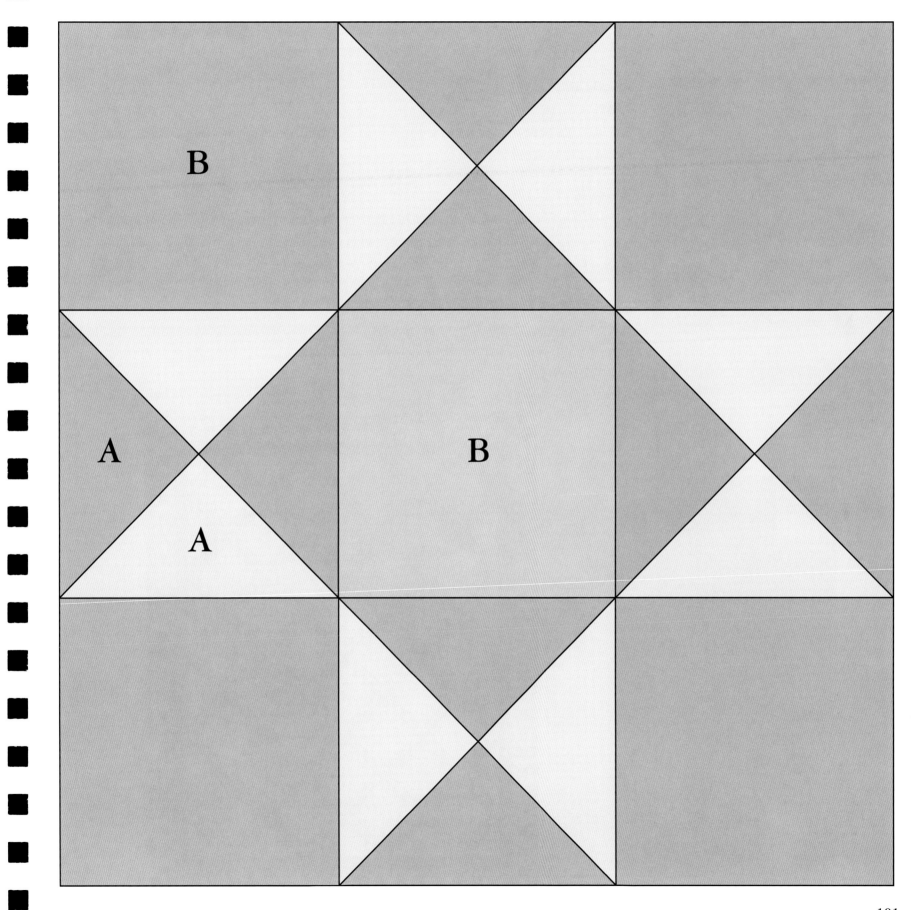

London Square

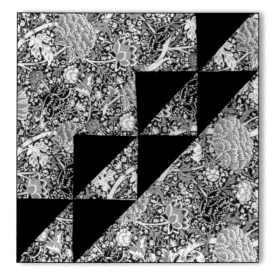

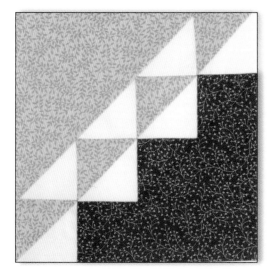

BLOCK
Cut

A: Cut 7, and cut 7 from contrasting fabric. B: Cut 2. (Variation: Use 3 fabrics, as shown in block at bottom left.)

Stitch

Stitch 7 A's to make a row, alternating fabrics. Make 2. (One row will begin and end with A; second row will begin and end with contrast A.) Stitch rows together, matching unlike fabrics. Stitch a B to either side of A's rows.

BLIMEY, IT'S A LONDON QUILT

Make 80 blocks, and stitch them together in 10 rows of 8 blocks as shown. Add inner border and sawtooth square border (see page 192). Finished size is about 84×112 inches.

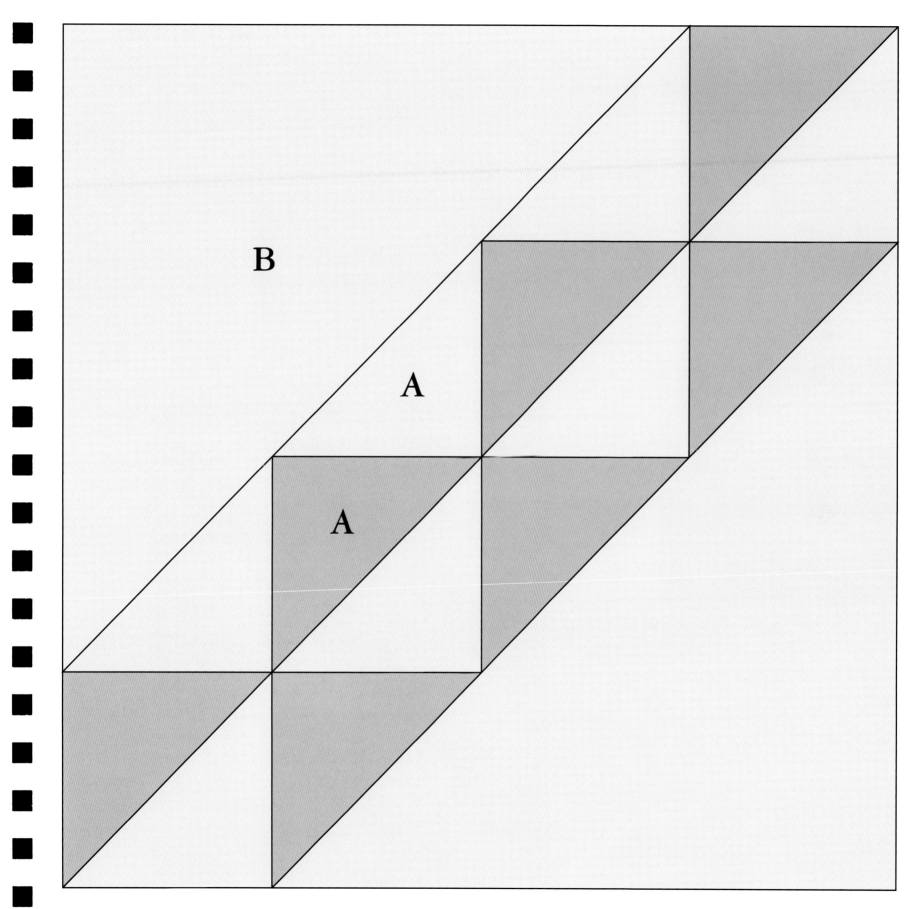

Log Cabin

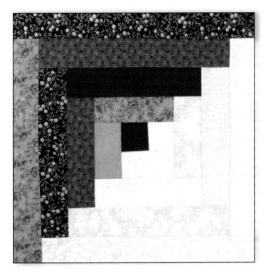

BLOCK

Cut

Cut 1 of each number.

Stitch

Stitch strips together in order; place them as shown on pattern.

CABIN WARMTH QUILT

Make 30 blocks, and stitch them together in 6 rows of 5 blocks. Add inner and outer borders. Finished size is about 50×59 inches.

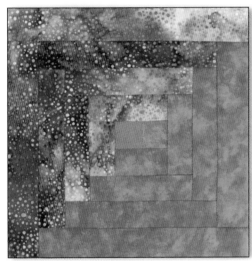

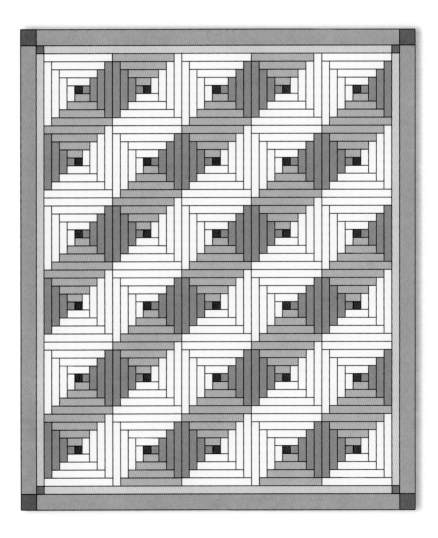

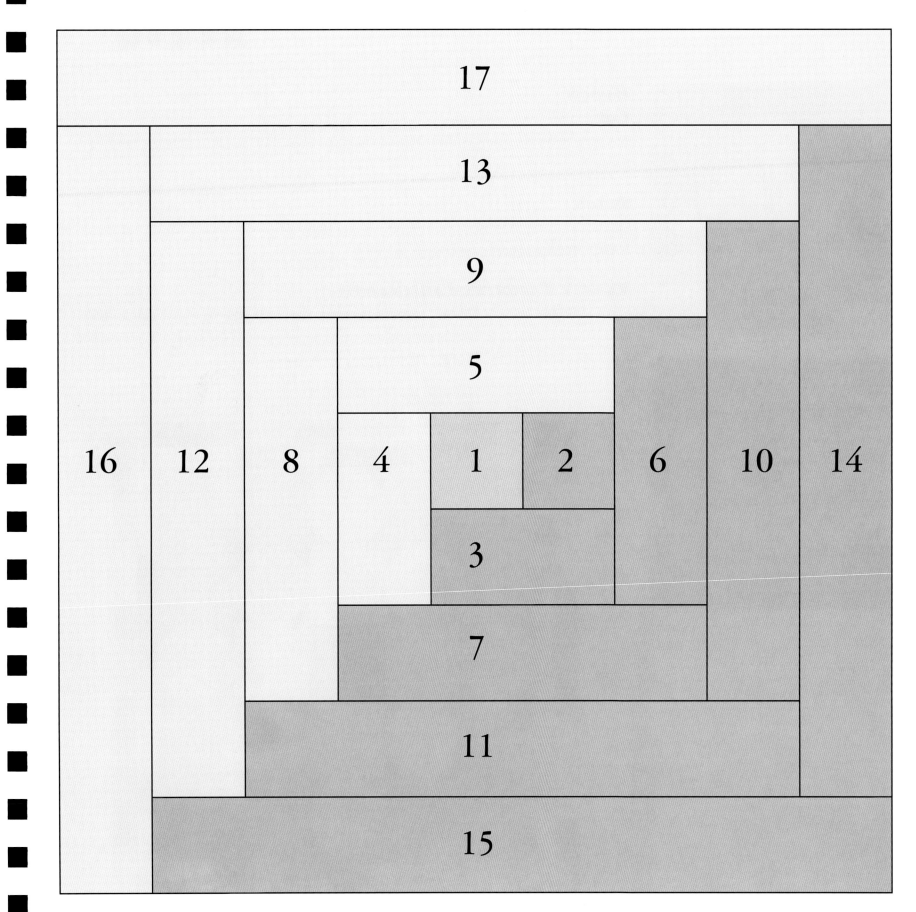

Kaleidoscope

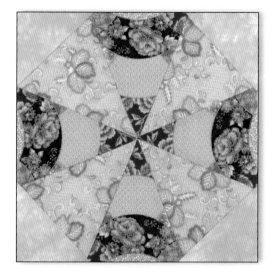

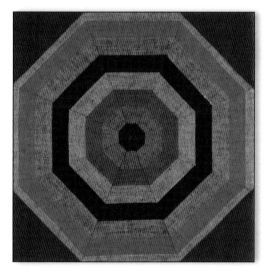

BLOCK
Cut

A: Cut 4, and cut 4 from contrasting fabric. (Variation: Cut all A's from same fabric.)
B: Cut 4.

Stitch

Stitch A to contrast A; make 4. Stitch AA's together to make octagon. Stitch a B to end of 4 A's to make a square and complete block.

FAMILY FAVORITE TABLECLOTH

Make 8 blocks, and cut 5 fabric squares. Also cut corner pieces to make a large quilt face. Stitch pieces together as shown, and add bricks border (see page 181). Finished size is about 49 inches square.

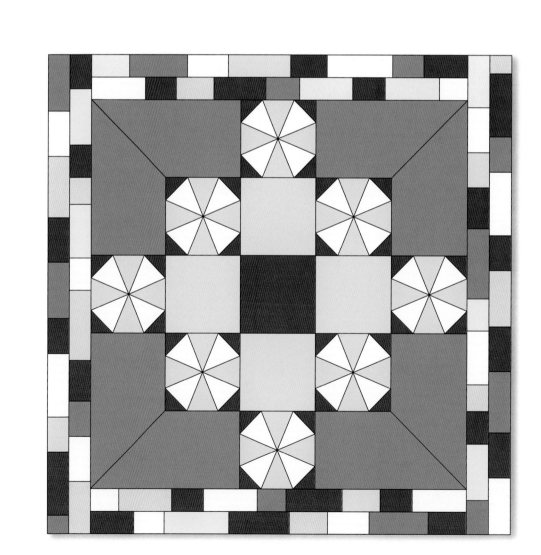

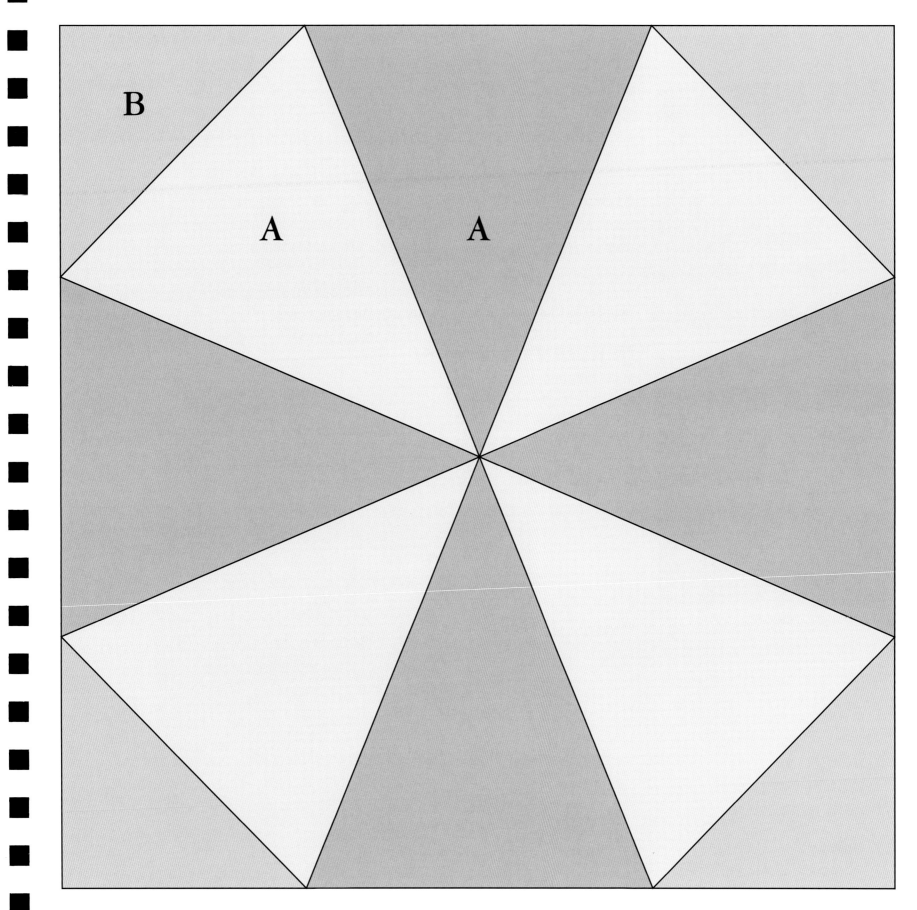

Friendship Star (Variation)

BLOCK

Cut

A: Cut 8, and cut 8 from contrasting fabric. B: Cut 4, and cut 4 from contrasting fabric. C: Cut 1.

Stitch

Stitch A to contrast A; make 8. Stitch AA to AA, matching unlike fabrics, to make 4-patch; make 4. Stitch B to contrast B; make 4. Stitch 4-patch to BB; stitch 4-patch to other side of BB. Make 2. Stitch BB to C; stitch BB to other side of C (make sure contrast B's are next to C). Sew rows together to complete block. Be sure to pay attention to placement of contrast B's when stitching rows together.

QUILTED FRIENDSHIP

Make 80 blocks, and stitch them together in 10 rows of 8 blocks. Add sashing and double outer border. Finished size is about 83×113 inches.

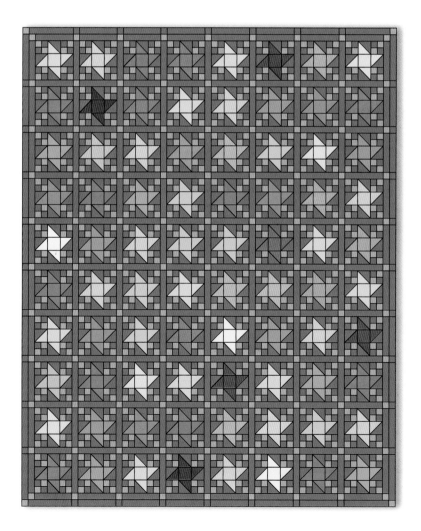

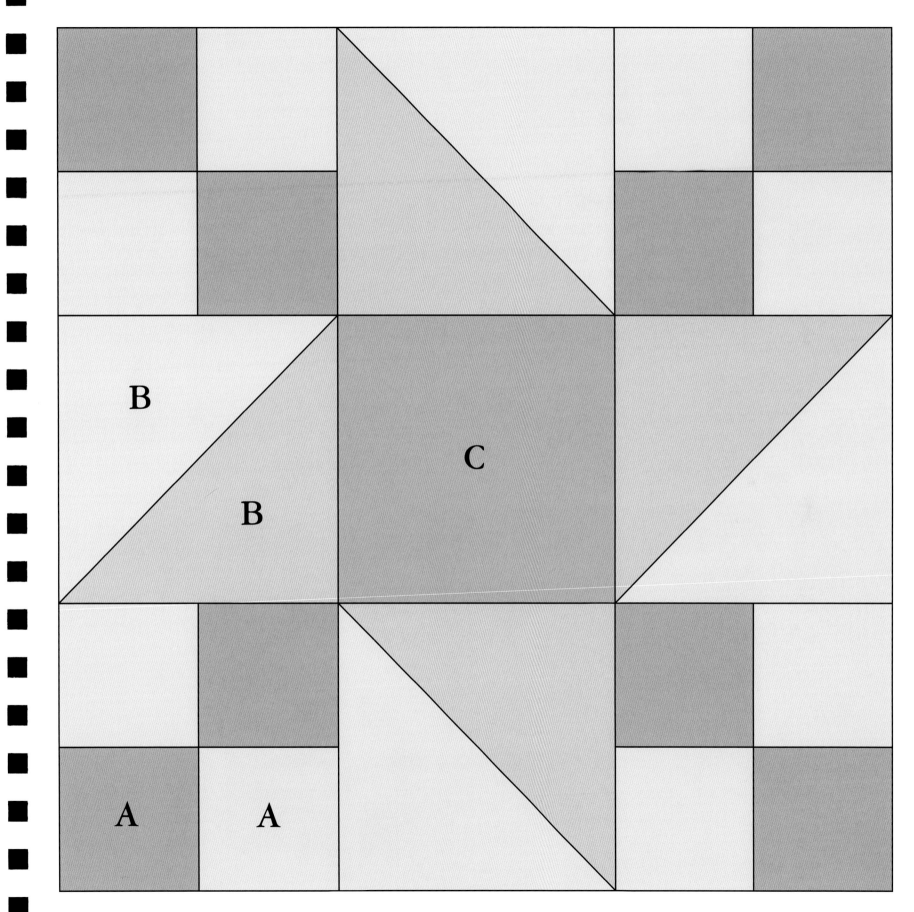

Four Corner Flowers

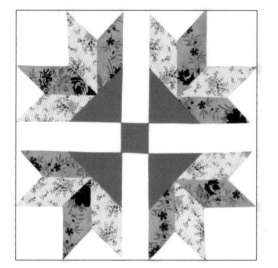

BLOCK

Cut

A: Cut 4. B: Cut 8, and cut 8 from reverse pattern. (Variation: Reverse B's can be a contrast fabric.) C: Cut 8. D: Cut 4. E: Cut 1. F: Cut 4.

Stitch

Stitch B to reverse B; make 8. Stitch C to BB; make 8. Stitch BBC to BBC (petals); make 4. Stitch D to petals; make 4. Stitch A to petals to make flower block; make 4. Stitch F to E; stitch F to other side of E. Stitch flower block to F; stitch flower block to other side of F. Make 2. Stitch FEF to bottom of flower block row and to top of other flower block row.

FREQUENT FLOWERS TOTE

Make 1 block, and stitch it to the front of a tote for real appeal. Finished size depends on size of tote.

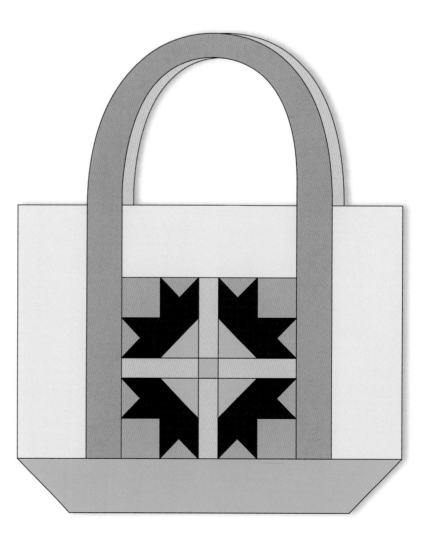

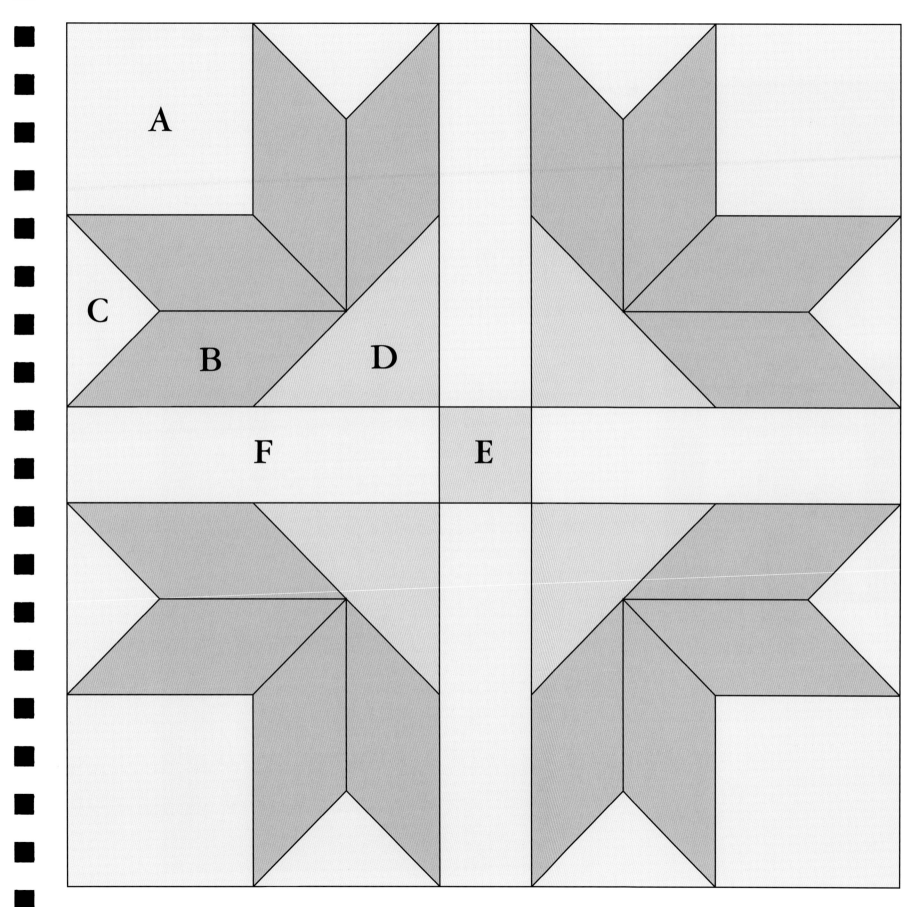

Flying Geese (Variation)

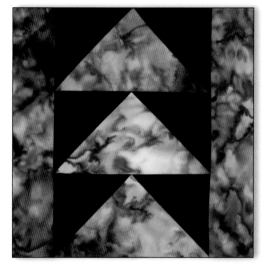

BLOCK

Cut

A: Cut 6. B: Cut 3. C: Cut 2.

Stitch

Sew A to short side of B, then sew A to other side of B. Make 3. Sew ABA pieces together. Sew a C to either side to complete block.

FLYING GEESE QUILT

Make 80 blocks, and stitch them together as shown in 10 rows of 8 blocks each. Add double border. Finished size is about 83×101 inches.

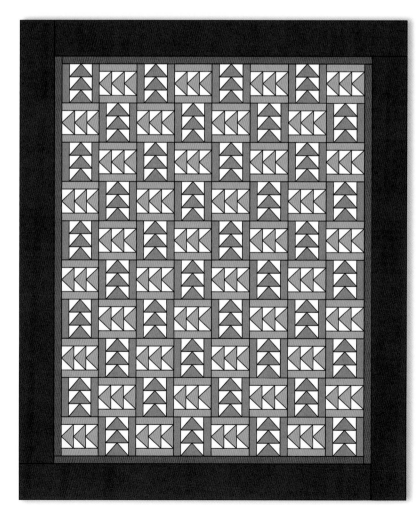

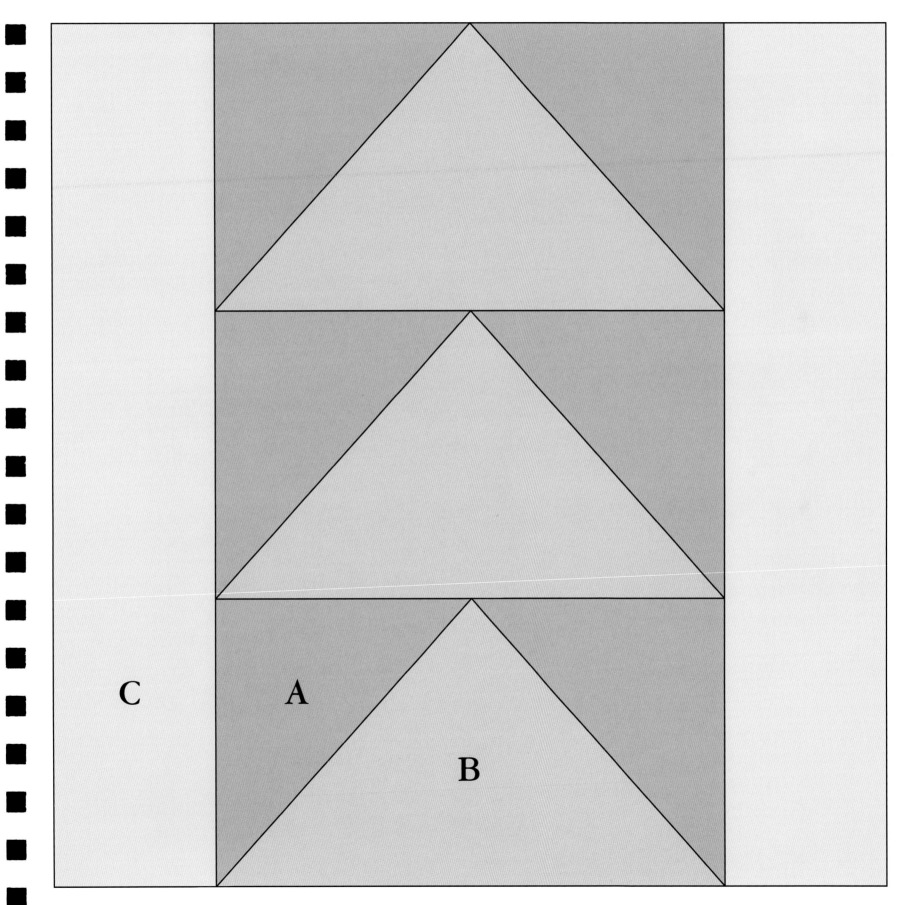

C

A

B

Double Pinwheel

BLOCK

Cut

A: Cut 4, and cut 4 from contrasting fabric. B: Cut 4.

Stitch

Stitch A to contrast A; make 4. Stitch AA to B on long edges; make 4. Stitch squares together to complete block.

TWIRLING QUILT

Make 32 blocks, and stitch them together as shown. Cut and stitch triangles to make quilt face. Add border. Finished size is about 56×69 inches.

114

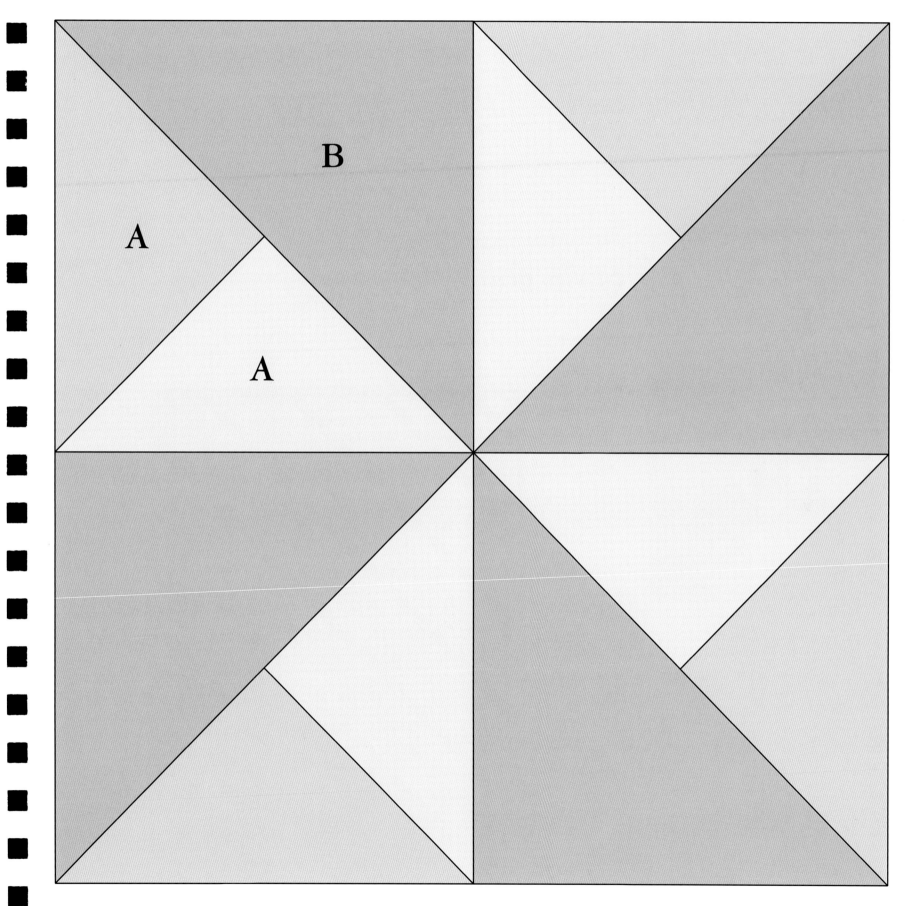

Cross

BLOCK

Cut

A: Cut 4. B: Cut 4. C: Cut 4. D: Cut 1.

Stitch

Stitch A to B; stitch A to other side of B. Make 2. Stitch a C to each side of D to make center square. Stitch B to center square; stitch B to other side of center square. Stitch rows together to complete block.

CROSSED QUILT

Make 40 blocks, and cut 40 fabric squares. Stitch them together as shown. Add blocks border. Finished size is about 74×92 inches.

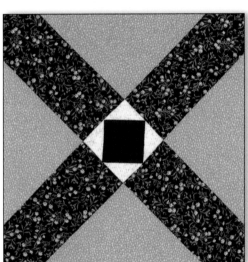

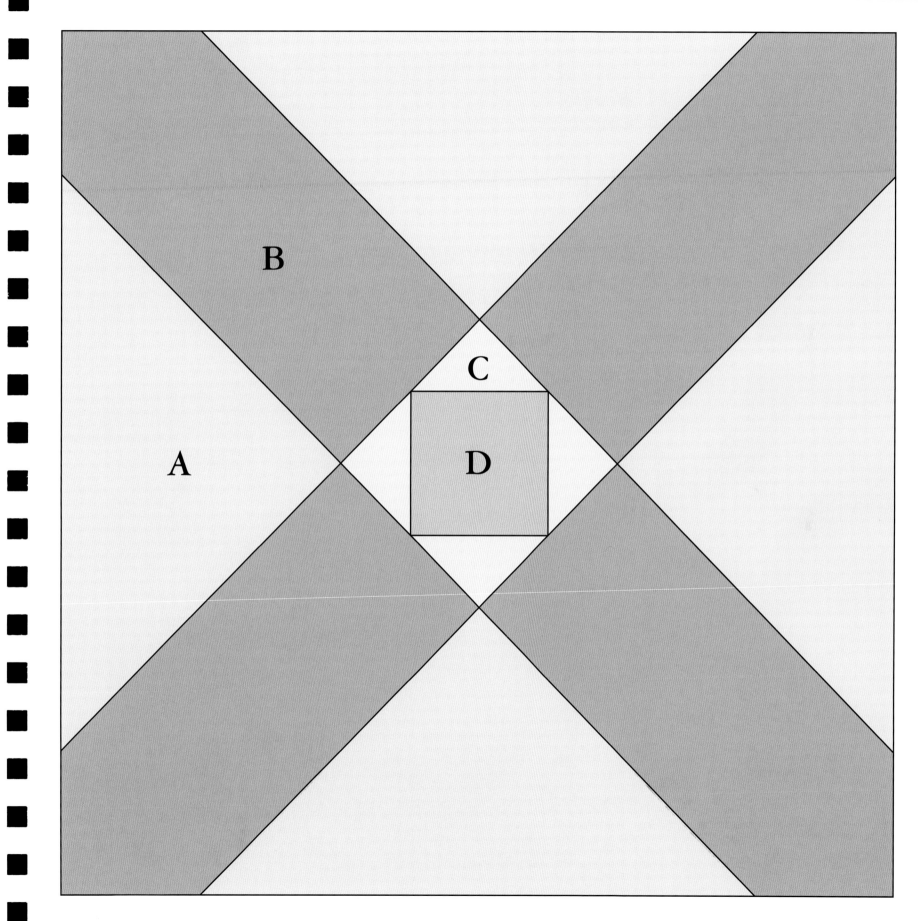

Friendship Circle

BLOCK
Cut
A: Cut 2. B: Cut 2. C: Cut 1.

Stitch
Stitch A to B; make 2. Stitch AB to C, and stitch BA to other side of C to complete block.

LINES OF FRIENDSHIP QUILT
Make 16 blocks, and stitch them together in 4 rows of 4 blocks as shown. Add border. Finished size is about 40 inches square.

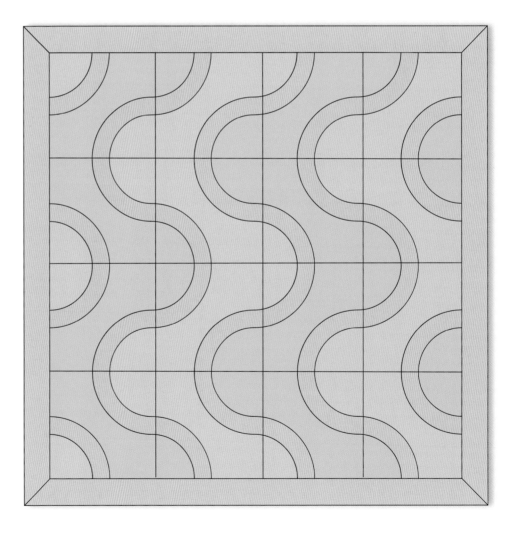

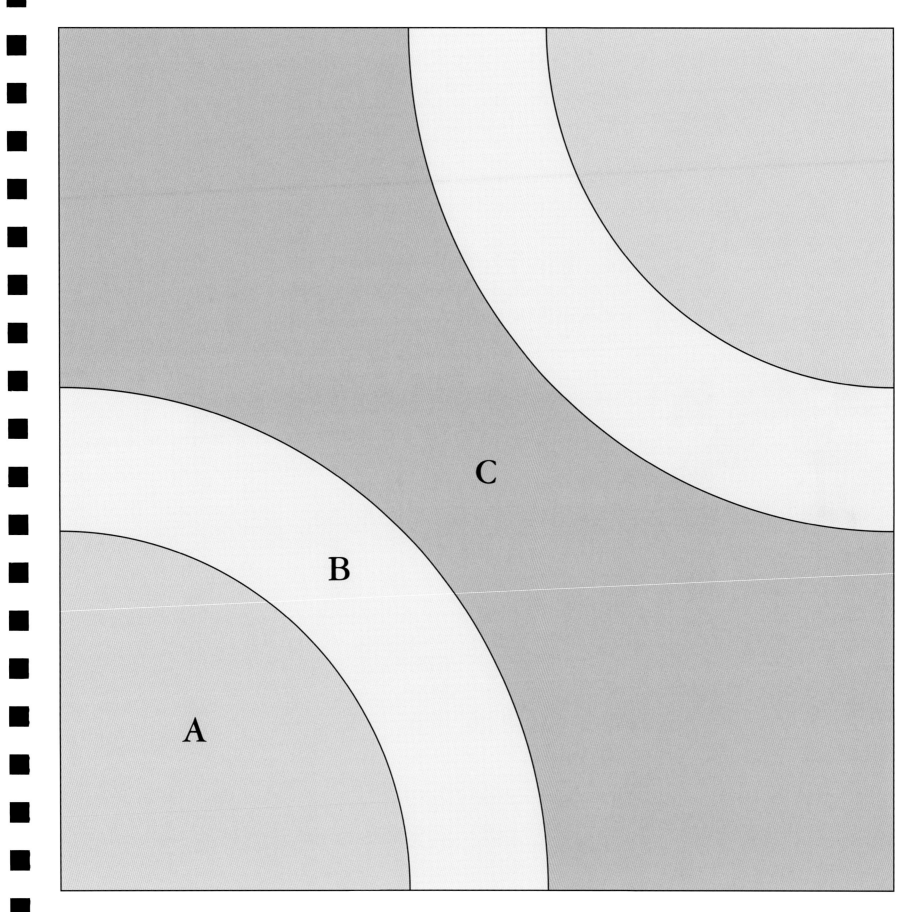

Chinese Fan

BLOCK

Cut

A: Cut 12, and cut 4 from contrasting fabric. B: Cut 16.

Stitch

Stitch A to B; make 16. Place all squares on table corresponding to pattern. Stitch squares together in rows, and then stitch rows together to complete block.

COZY CAFÉ FAN CURTAINS

Make the number of blocks needed for width of curtain. Stitch blocks together in a row, and stitch top and bottom fabric to desired length for curtain. Finished size depends on length and width of curtain needed.

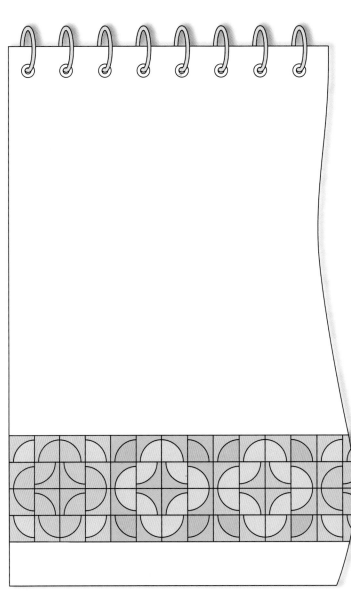

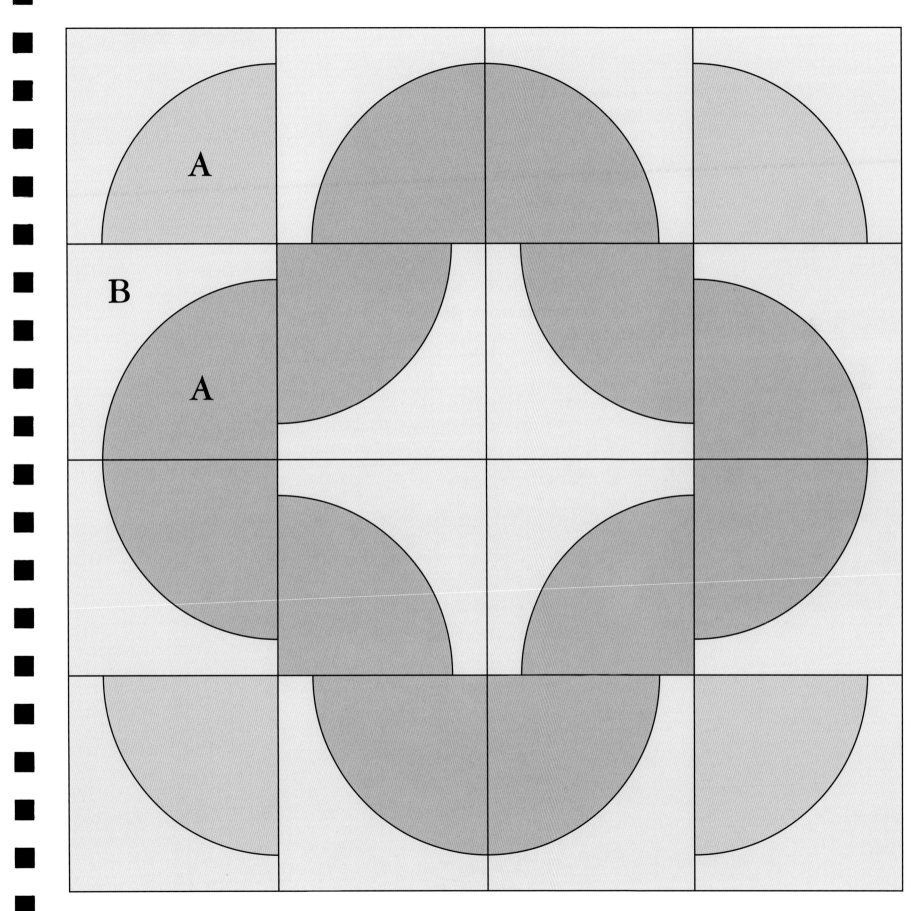

Chain (Variation)

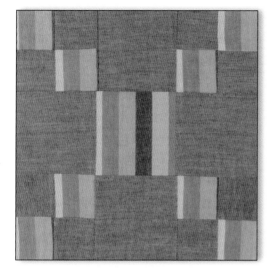

BLOCK

Cut

A: Cut 8, and cut 8 from contrasting fabric. B: Cut 4, and cut 1 from contrasting fabric.

Stitch

Stitch A to contrast A; make 8. Stitch AA to AA, matching unlike fabrics, to create 4-patch. Make 4. Stitch 4-patch to B, then stitch 4-patch to other side of B. Make 2. Stitch B to contrast B, then stitch B to other side of contrast B. Sew rows together to complete block. (Make sure contrast B's are in 4 corners of square.)

CHAINED MEDLEY QUILT

Make 18 blocks, and cut 17 fabric squares. Stitch them together as shown. Add bars and blocks border (see page 189). Finished size is about 48×59 inches.

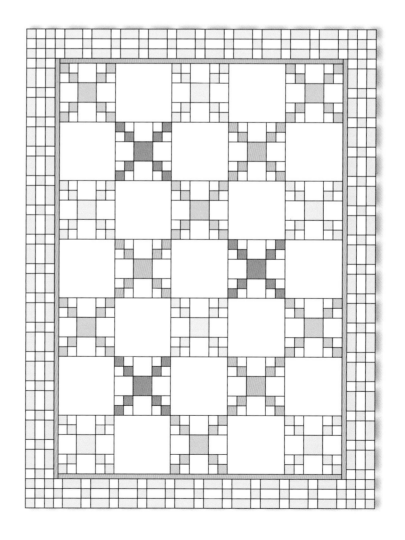

A A

B

B

Card Trick

BLOCK
Cut
From 4 contrast fabrics: A: Cut 2. B: Cut 2. From background fabric: A: Cut 4. B: Cut 4.

Stitch
Place all pieces on table as shown on pattern. Stitch center B's together. Stitch background A to contrast A; make 4. Stitch background B to contrast B; make 4. Stitch AA to corresponding BB; make 4. Stitch contrast A to corresponding AABB; make 4. Stitch pieces together and to center square, matching fabrics, to complete block.

CARD TRICK COUCH COZY
Make 2 blocks, and add borders to each. Sew blocks to a length of fabric to create pockets on either side. Finished size depends on length of fabric used to fit couch.

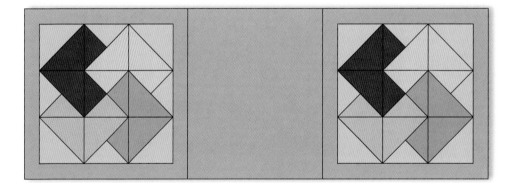

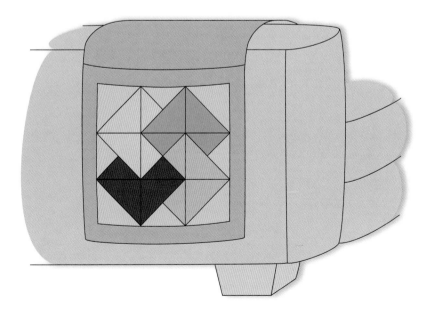

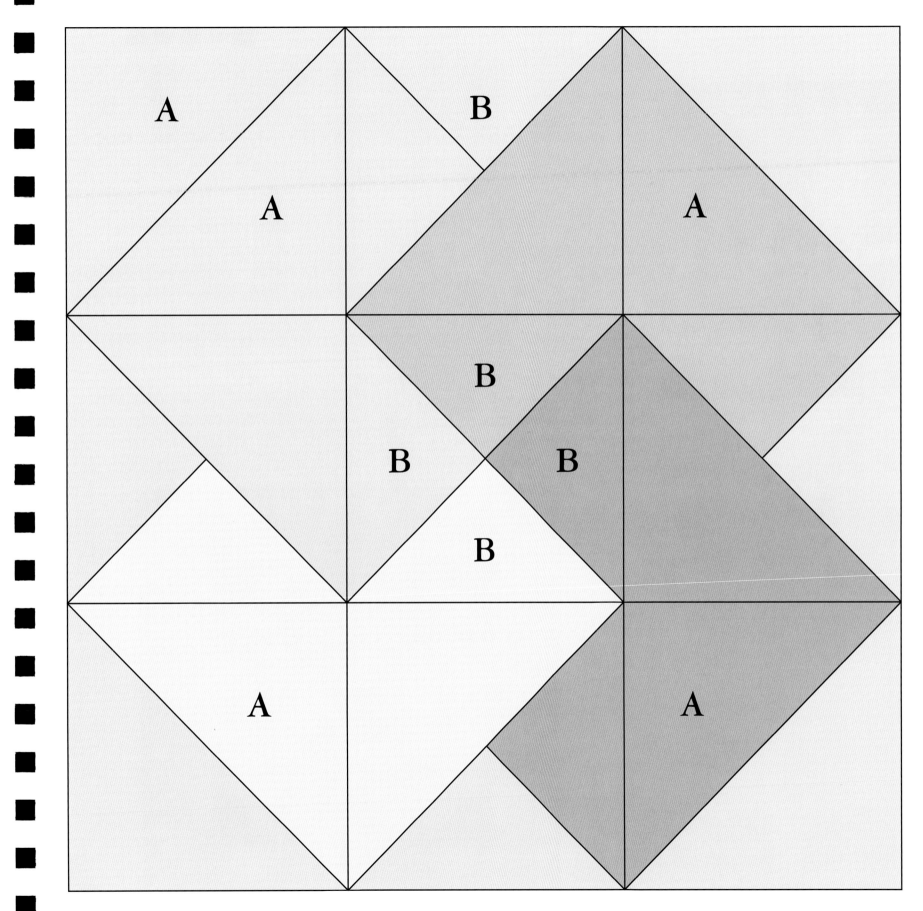

Basket

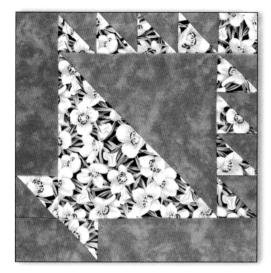

BLOCK

Cut

A: Cut 10, and cut 10 from contrasting fabric. B: Cut 9, and cut 1 from contrasting fabric. C: Cut 1, and cut 1 from contrasting fabric. (Variation: For basket different from handle, cut 1 C and 2 A's from a second contrast fabric.)

Stitch

Stitch A to contrast A; make 10. Stitch 4 AA squares together in a sawtooth pattern; make 2. To one AA row, stitch B to 1 end and stitch contrast B to other end. Stitch AA to 3 B's in a row, matching unlike fabrics with AA square. Stitch B to AA square, matching like fabrics, then stitch 4 B's to other side of AA. Stitch C to contrast C on long edge. Stitch rows around center square as shown in pattern to complete block.

DINNER BASKET TABLECLOTH

Make 4 basket blocks and 1 chain variation block (see page 122). Cut 4 fabric squares. Sew them together as shown. Add inner border and outer flying geese border (see page 184). Finished size is about 28 inches square.

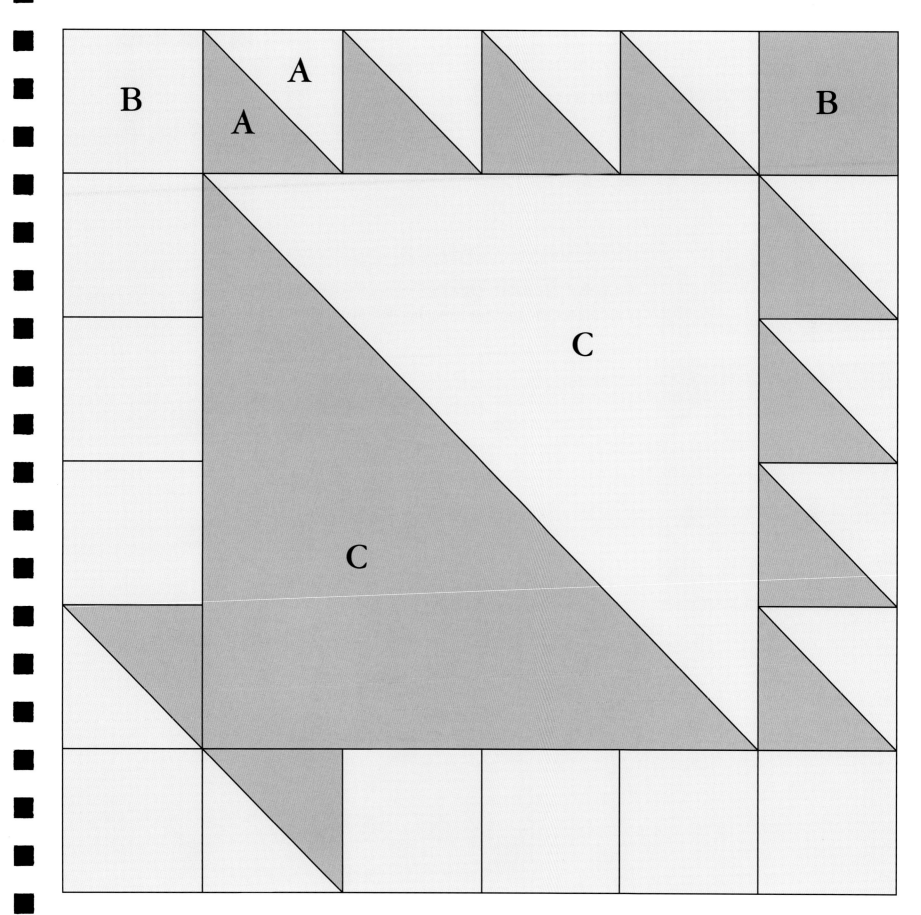

Album Block

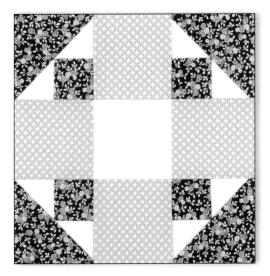

BLOCK

Cut

A: Cut 4. B: Cut 8. C: Cut 4. D: Cut 4, and cut 1 from contrasting fabric.

Stitch

Stitch B to A, then stitch B to other side of A. Make 4. Stitch C to BAB; make 4. Stitch D to contrast D, then stitch D to other side of contrast D. Stitch CBAB to D, then stitch CBAB to other side of D. Make 2. Stitch rows together to complete block.

FAMILY ALBUM QUILT

Make 12 blocks, and stitch them together in 4 rows of 3 blocks each. Add wide sashing and flying geese border (see page 184). Finished size is about 33×54 inches.

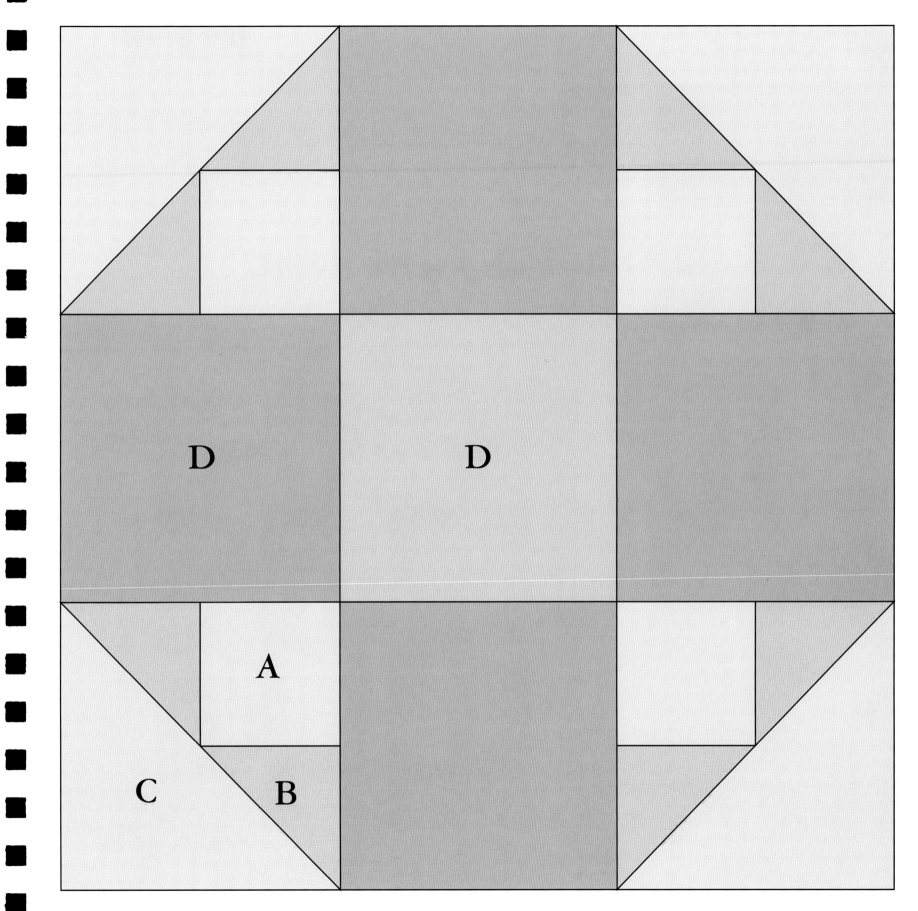

Rail Fence

BLOCK

Cut

A: Cut 4 from 3 different fabrics.

Stitch

Selecting an A from each fabric, stitch A to A to A; make 4. Always stitch fabrics in same order. Stitch squares together as shown in pattern to complete block.

FENCED FAMILY ROOM WALL HANGING

Make 9 blocks, and stitch them together in 3 rows of 3 blocks each. Add churn dash border (see page 188). Finished size is about 30 inches square.

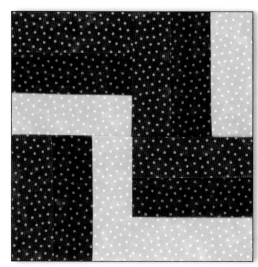

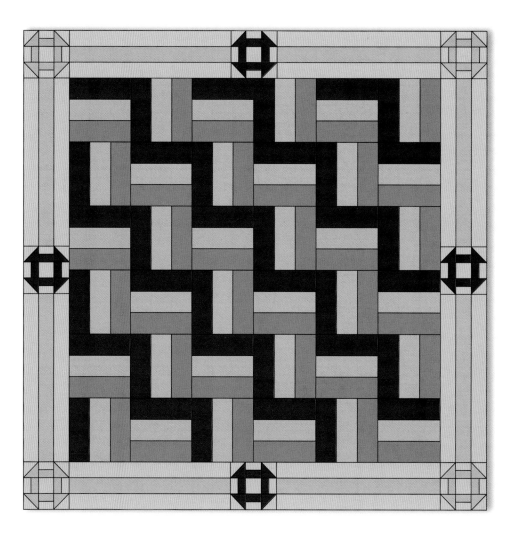

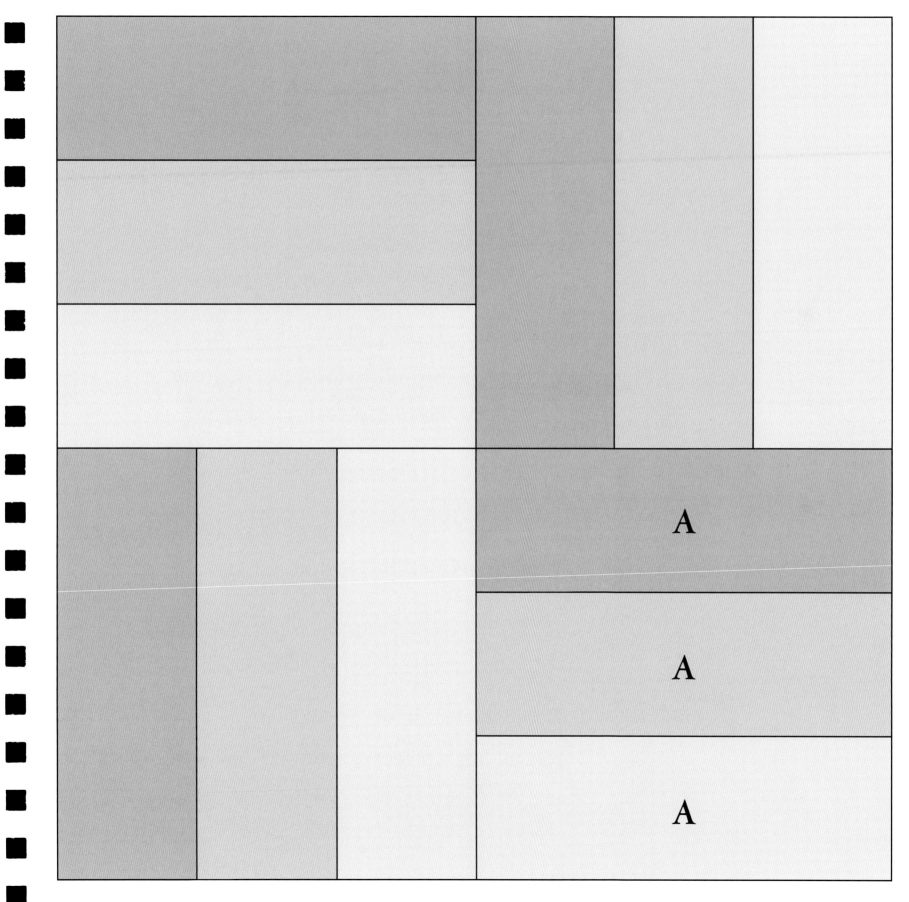

Fresh from the Garden

Is there a more peaceful way to relax than sitting

in a garden, smelling the flowers, reveling in all the colors,

and listening to the buzzing and chirping of creatures

all around you? There truly is no better place to be on a

sunny spring day! Now you can enjoy the pleasures

of the outdoors even in the middle of a long, cold winter—

make a quilt that will evoke all those special joys.

Make a profusion of flower blocks, or craft a few whimsical

creature blocks. You'll find something in this chapter that

will delight every nature lover you know!

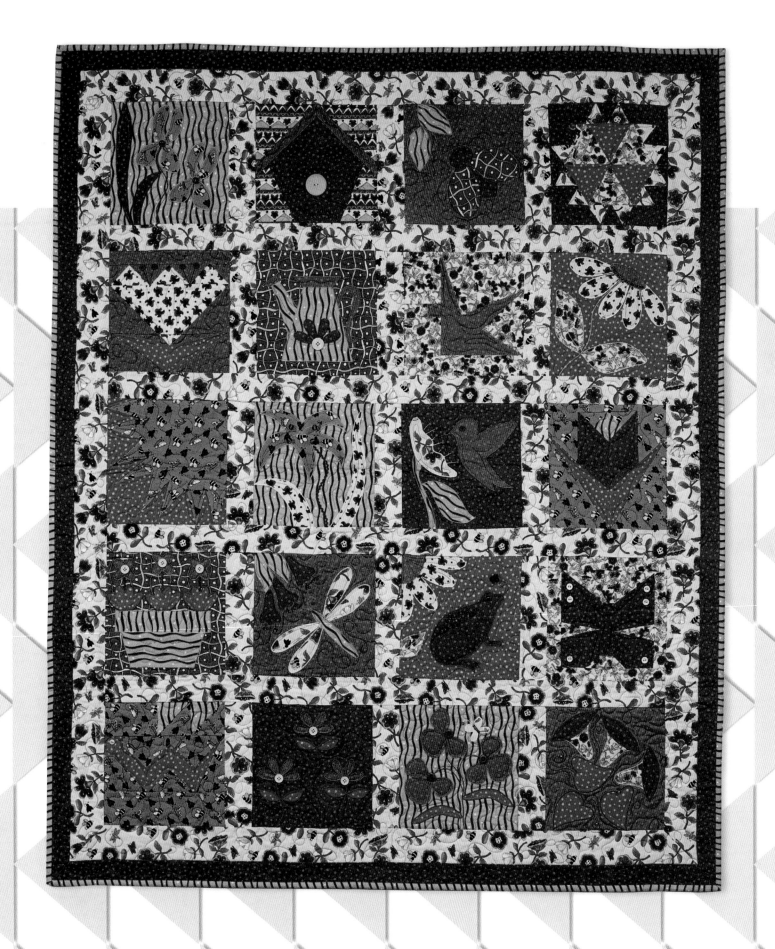

Wayward Daisy

BLOCK
Cut

Background: Cut 1. All other pieces: Fuse double-sided webbing to fabrics. Leaves: Cut 2. Petals: Cut 5. Flower center: Cut 1. (Do not add seam allowances to fused pieces.)

Stitch

Place and fuse all pieces. By machine, appliqué all fused pieces using narrow zigzag stitch. Use same stitch to make flower veins and stem. (Variation: Hand-stitch thin cord to fabric for stem.) Sew beads around bottom of flower center.

DAISY QUILT

Make 36 blocks, and cut 36 fabric squares. Stitch them together as shown, adding sashing and border. Finished size is about 87×97 inches.

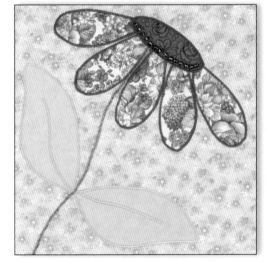

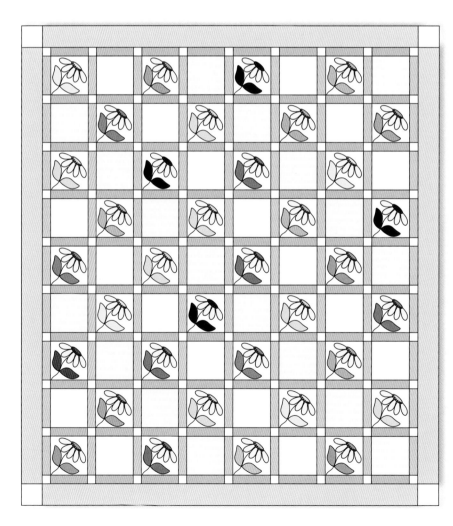

Watering Can

BLOCK

Cut

Background: Cut 1. All other pieces: Fuse double-sided webbing to fabrics. Watering can pieces: Cut 1 each. Flower petals: Cut 4. (Do not add seam allowances to fused pieces.)

Stitch

Place and fuse all pieces. By machine, appliqué all fused pieces using a narrow zigzag stitch. Sew a large button to bottom of petals.

FRESHLY WATERED PILLOW

Make 1 block. Add blocks and bars border (see page 180) to fit pillow form. Finished size depends on size of pillow form.

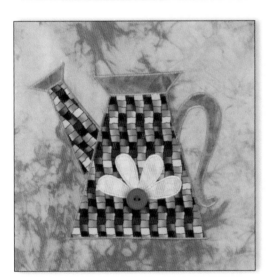

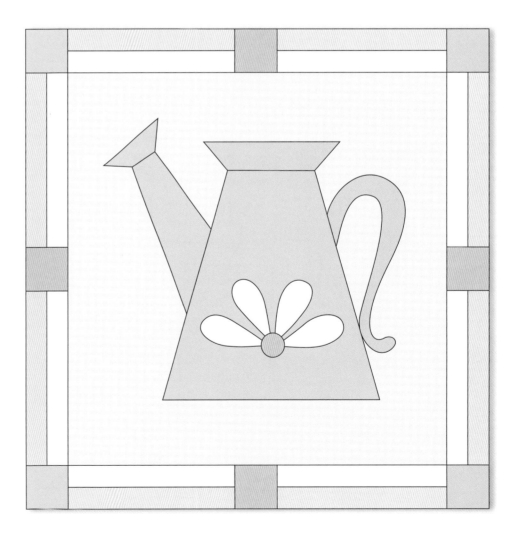

Trumpeting Tulip

BLOCK

Cut

A–D: Cut 1, and cut 1 from reverse pattern. E: Cut 2. F: Cut 1. G: Cut 1.

Stitch

Stitch A to B. Make 2 (1 is reverse pattern). Stitch AB to BA, with leaves pointing outward. Stitch E to F, and stitch E to other side of F. Stitch G to top of EFE. Stitch D to D, and then stitch EFEG to top of DD. Stitch a C to either side of this piece. Stitch this piece to top of ABBA to complete block.

TULIP MORNING PLACE MAT

Make 1 block, and add top and bottom borders and wide side borders. Finished size is about 19×15 inches.

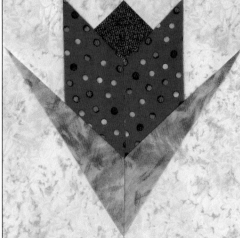

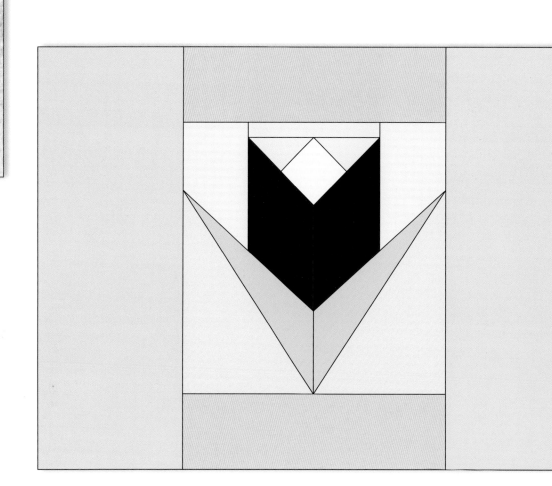

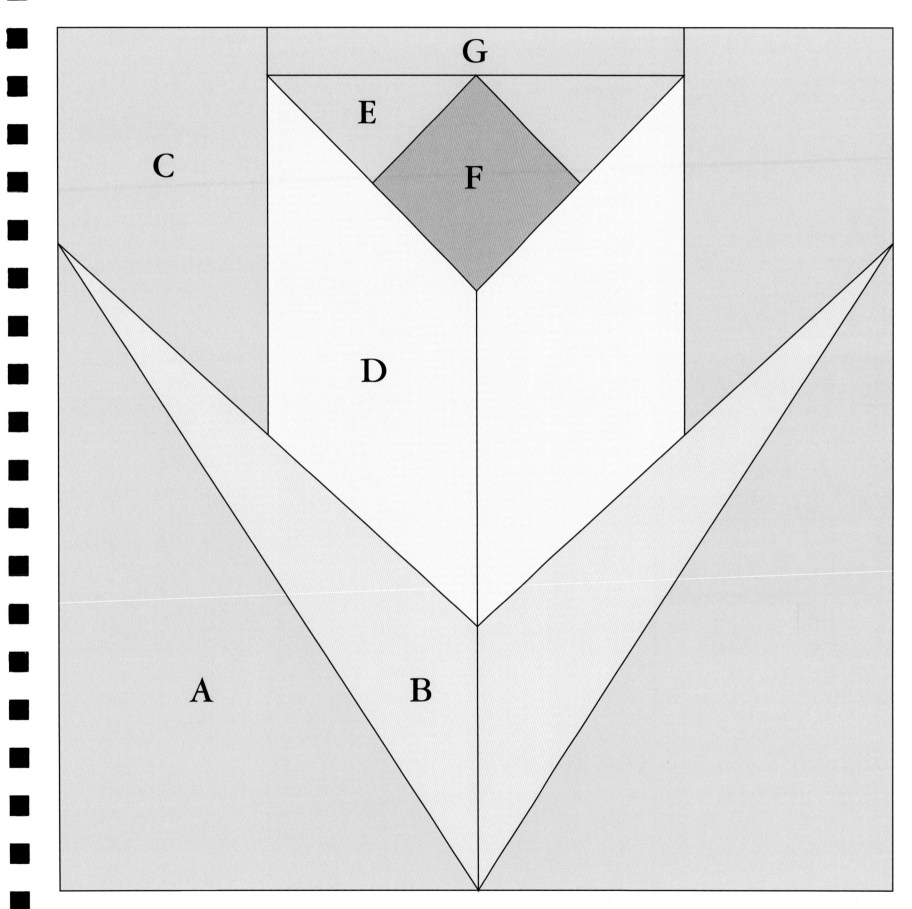

Sunshine Day

BLOCK

Cut

A: Cut 1. B: Cut 4. C: Cut 4. D: Cut 1, and cut 1 from reverse pattern. E: Cut 2. F: Cut 1, and cut 1 from reverse pattern. G: Cut 1, and cut 1 from reverse pattern. H: Cut 1.

Stitch

Stitch D to B, then stitch E to other side of B. Stitch B to other side of E, and stitch F to other side of B. Make 2. Stitch C to G, and stitch another C to other side of G. Make 2. Stitch H to CGC, and stitch reverse CGC to other side of H. Stitch DBEBF to one side of this piece, and stitch other DBEBF to other side (rays). Stitch rays to A.

SUNSHINE WALL HANGING

Make 4 blocks, and stitch together as shown. Add double picture frame border (see page 178). Finished size is about 27 inches square.

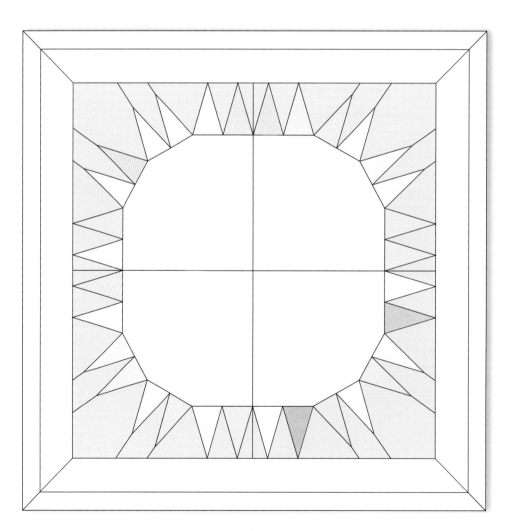

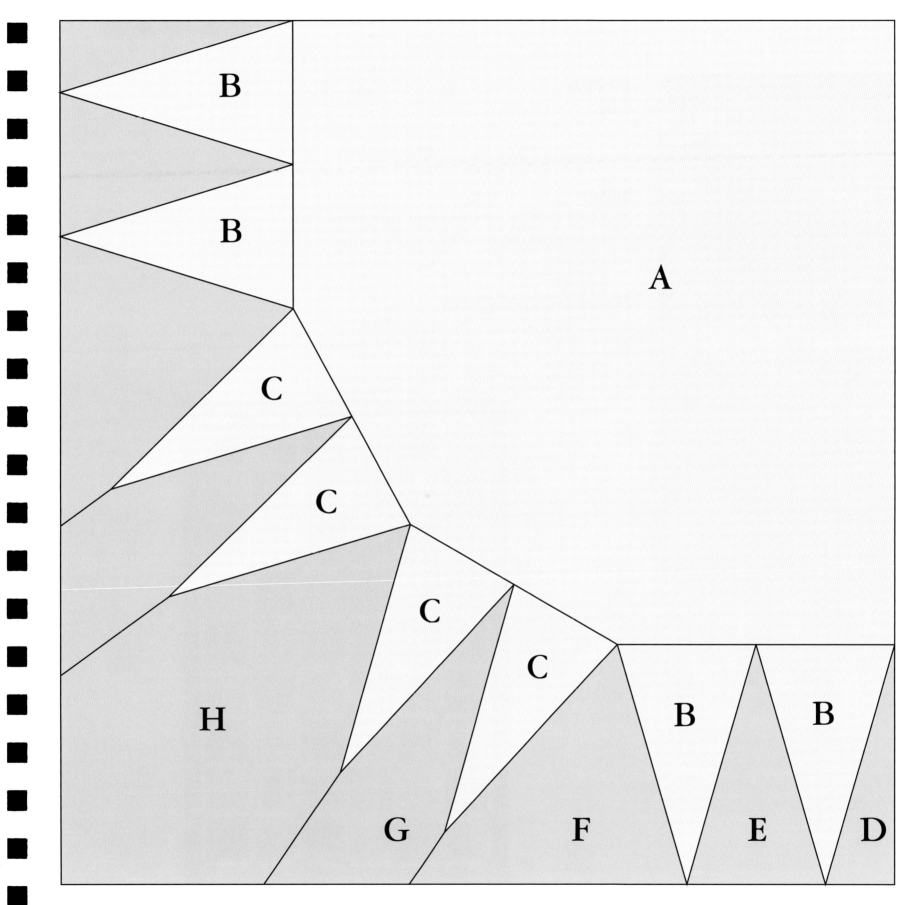

Flying High

BLOCK
Cut

Background: Cut 1. All other pieces: Fuse double-sided webbing to fabrics, and cut 1 each. (Do not add seam allowances to fused pieces.)

Stitch

Place and fuse all pieces. By machine, appliqué all fused pieces using narrow zigzag stitch. Use same stitch to make leaf vein and frog's tongue. Sew large and small beads to back of frog. Sew insect button above tongue, and add button for frog's eye.

HIGH FLYING QUILT

Make 27 blocks, and cut 27 fabric squares. Sew them together as shown, adding sashing and outer border. Finished size is about 95×65 inches.

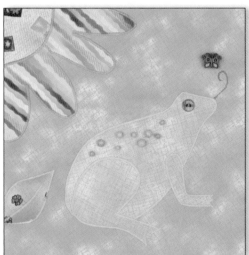

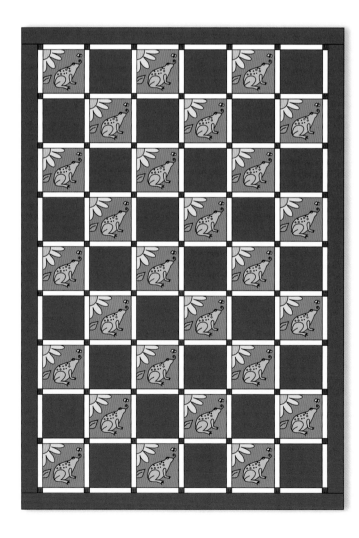

Sweet Nectar

BLOCK

Cut

Background: Cut 1. All other pieces: Fuse double-sided webbing to fabrics, and cut 1 each. (Do not add seam allowances to fused pieces.)

Stitch

Place and fuse all pieces. By machine, appliqué all fused pieces using narrow zigzag stitch. Use same stitch to make flower stamen, leaf vein, and bird's beak. Sew beads to ends of stamen, and sew on button for hummingbird eye.

SWEETEST PILLOW

Make 1 block. Add a thin inner border and rambling leaves border (see page 177). Finished size is about 17 inches square.

Summer Sunflower

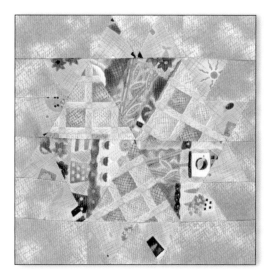

BLOCK

Cut

A: Cut 3, and cut 3 from contrasting fabric. B: Cut 2, and cut 2 from reverse pattern. C: Cut 12, and cut 2 from background fabric. D: Cut 4. E: Cut 2, and cut 2 from reverse pattern. F: Cut 2, and cut 2 from reverse pattern.

Stitch

Stitch A to contrast A, and stitch A to other side of contrast A. Stitch contrast A to A, and stitch contrast A to other side of A. Stitch B to C, stitch background C to other side of C, stitch C to other side of background C, and stitch reverse B to C. Make 2. Stitch D to BCCCB, and stitch D to other side. Make 2. Stitch E to C, stitch F to other side of C, stitch C to other side of F. Make 4 (2 are reverse pattern). Stitch an ECFC to each side of AAA. Make 2. Stitch rows together to complete block.

SUNFLOWER TABLE RUNNER

Make 3 blocks, and cut 2 fabric squares. Stitch them together as shown. Add sashing between blocks and triangles on ends. Add jagged edge border (see page 191). Finished size is about 65×15 inches.

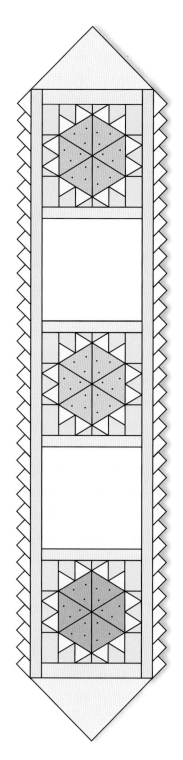

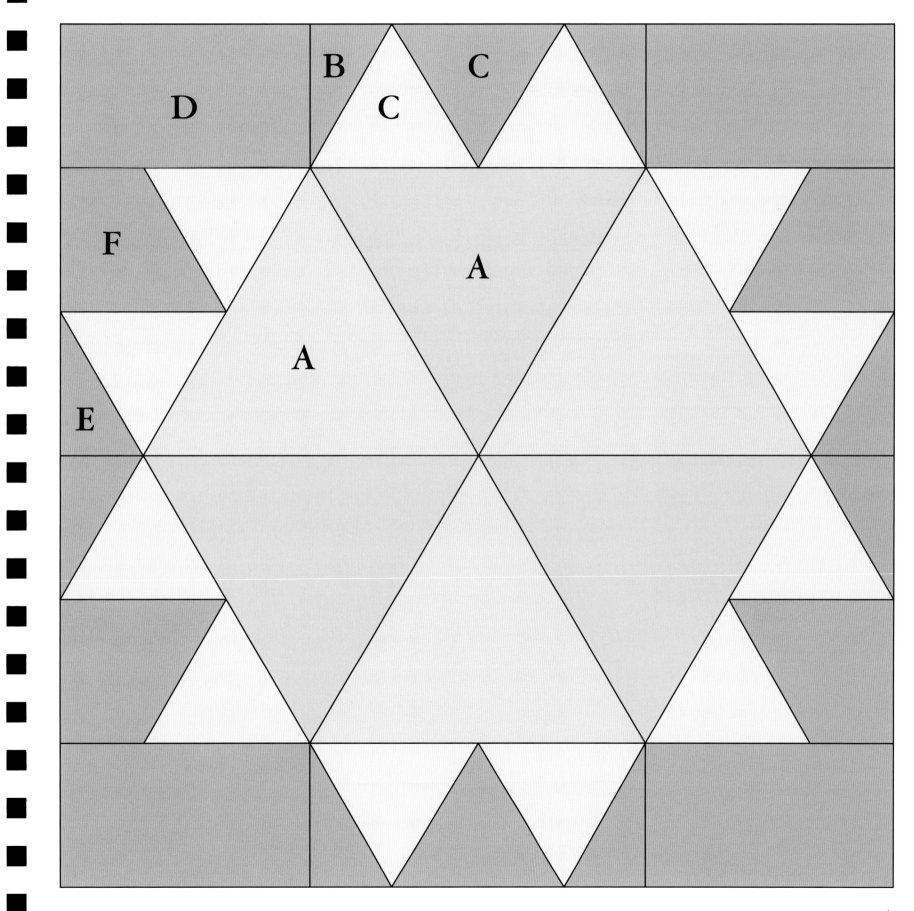

Pretty Maids

BLOCK
Cut

Background: Cut 1. All other pieces: Fuse double-sided webbing to fabrics. Leaves: Cut 6. Petals: Cut 12. (Do not add seam allowances to fused pieces.)

Stitch

Place and fuse all pieces. By machine, appliqué all fused pieces using narrow zigzag stitch. Hand-stitch narrow cord on background for flower stems. Sew buttons to middle of flowers.

PRETTY MAIDS TEA COZY

Make 1 block, and round off top corners. Stitch block to the front of a purchased tea cozy. Finished size depends on size of cozy.

My Favorite Flower

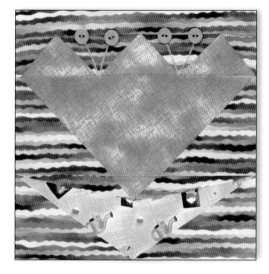

BLOCK

Cut

A: Cut 1. B: Cut 2. C: Cut 3, and cut 2 from background fabric. D: Cut 2. E: Cut 1. F: Cut 1, and cut 1 from reverse pattern. G: Cut 1. H: Cut 1, and cut 1 from reverse pattern. I: Cut 1, and cut 1 from reverse pattern.

Stitch

Stitch C's to background C's, alternating fabrics. Stitch a B to each end of C piece. Stitch D to E, and then stitch D to other side of E. Stitch F to G, and then stitch reverse F to other side of G. Stitch I to H. Make 2. Stitch IH to HI. Stitch FGF to top of IHHI. Sew rows together to complete block. Use a narrow zigzag stitch to make stamen, and sew a button to end of each.

WALL FLOWER HANGING

Make 4 blocks, and stitch them together as shown. Add sashing and diamond star squares border (see page 190). Finished size is about 29 inches square.

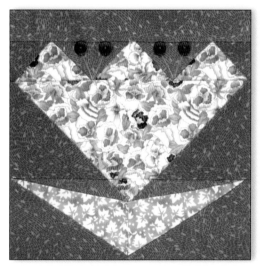

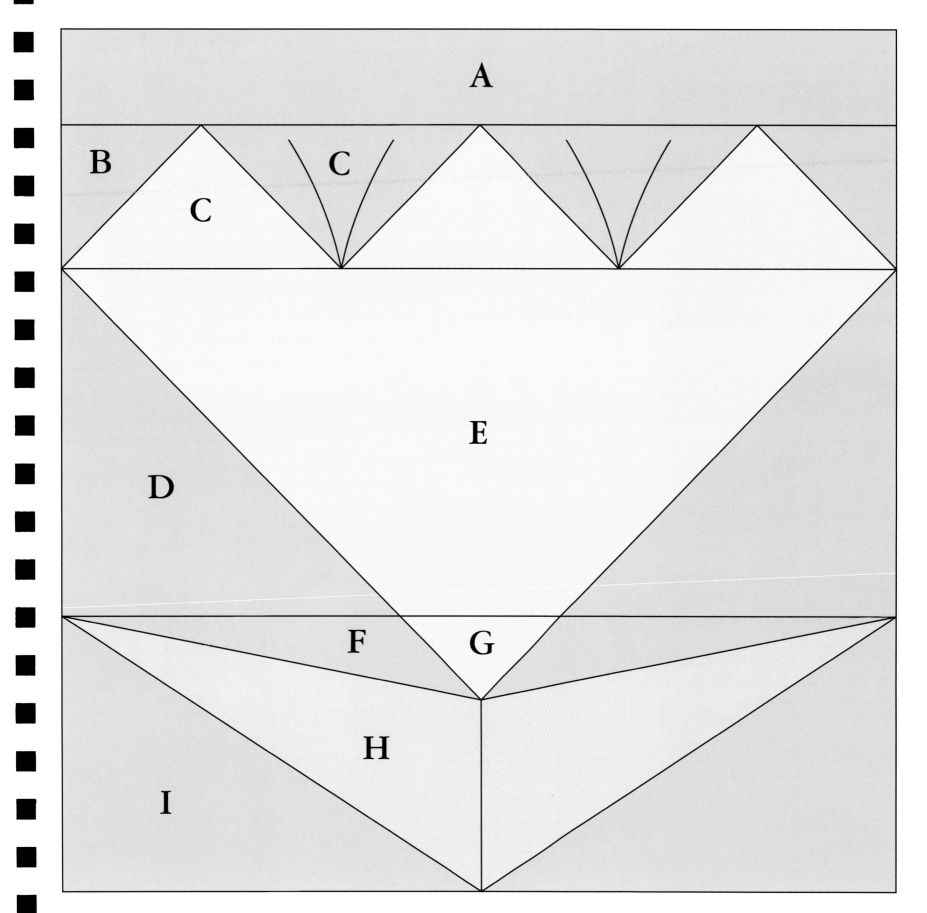

Fly Away Ladybug!

BLOCK

Cut

Background: Cut 1. All other pieces: Fuse double-sided webbing to fabrics. Leaves: Cut 2. Wings: Cut 2. Head, body: Cut 1 each. (Do not add seam allowances to fused pieces.)

Stitch

Place and fuse all pieces. By machine, appliqué all fused pieces using narrow zigzag stitch. Use same stitch to make ladybug antennae and leaf veins. Sew beads to end of antennae, and sew buttons to ladybug wings.

LADYBUG QUILT

Make 9 blocks, and sew together in 3 rows of 3 blocks, adding sashing. Sew on piano keys border (see page 182). Finished size is about 43 inches square.

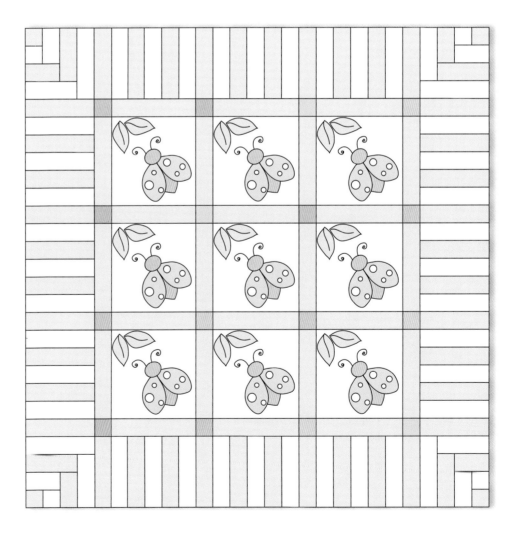

Peeping Out

BLOCK

Cut

Background: Cut 1. Ribbon or cording: Cut 3 pieces to needed lengths. All other pieces: Fuse double-sided webbing to fabrics. Pot pieces: Cut 1 each. Flowers, leaves: Cut 3 each. (Do not add seam allowances to fused pieces.)

Stitch

Place and fuse all pieces, being sure ends of ribbon are under flowers and leaves before fusing. By machine, appliqué all fused pieces using narrow zigzag stitch. Sew buttons to middle of flowers.

GARDENING APRON

Make 2 blocks and an extra flower and leaves. Sew blocks to apron for pockets, and fuse flower and leaves to front of apron. Finished size depends on size of apron.

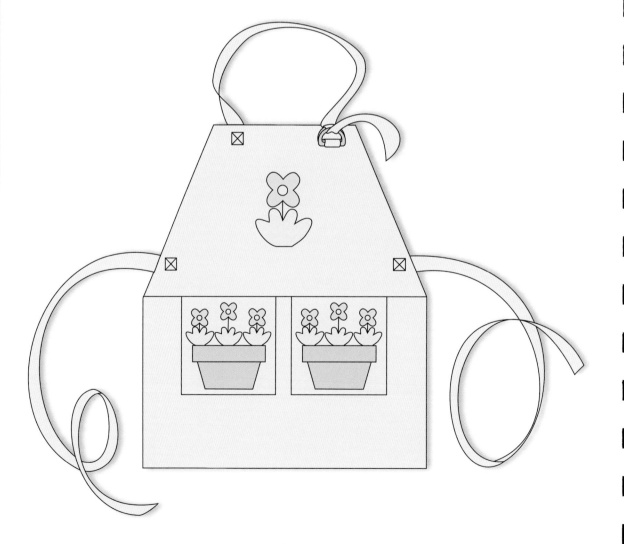

154

Inching Along

BLOCK

Cut

A: Cut 1. B: Cut 2, and cut 2 from background fabric. C–E: Cut 1 each. F–H: Cut 1, and cut 1 from reverse pattern. I–O: Cut 1 each.

Stitch

Stitch B to background B; make 2. Stitch BB to BB, alternating fabrics. Stitch A to left side of BBBB. Stitch C to top of D; stitch E to bottom of CD. Stitch F to G, and then stitch H to bottom of FG. Make 2 (1 is reverse pattern). Stitch I to J, and stitch K to bottom of IJ. Stitch N to M, and stitch L to bottom of NM. Stitch CDE to FGH, then stitch reverse FGH to other side. Stitch IJK to reverse FGH, and stitch NML to end. Stitch rows together (third row is piece O) to complete block. By machine, use narrow zigzag stitch to make antennae. Sew beads to ends of antennae, and sew on a button for eye.

CATERPILLAR PILLOW

Make 1 block, and add flying geese border (see page 184). Finished size is about 13 inches square.

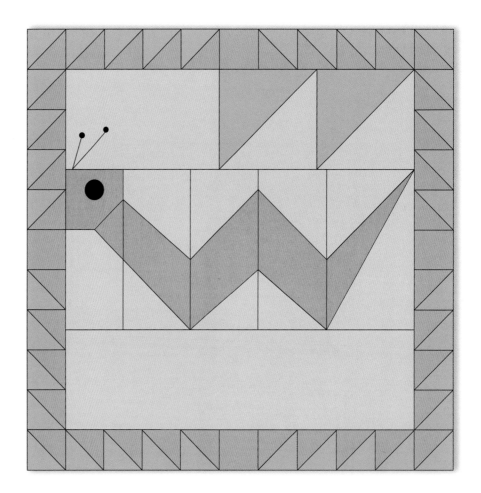

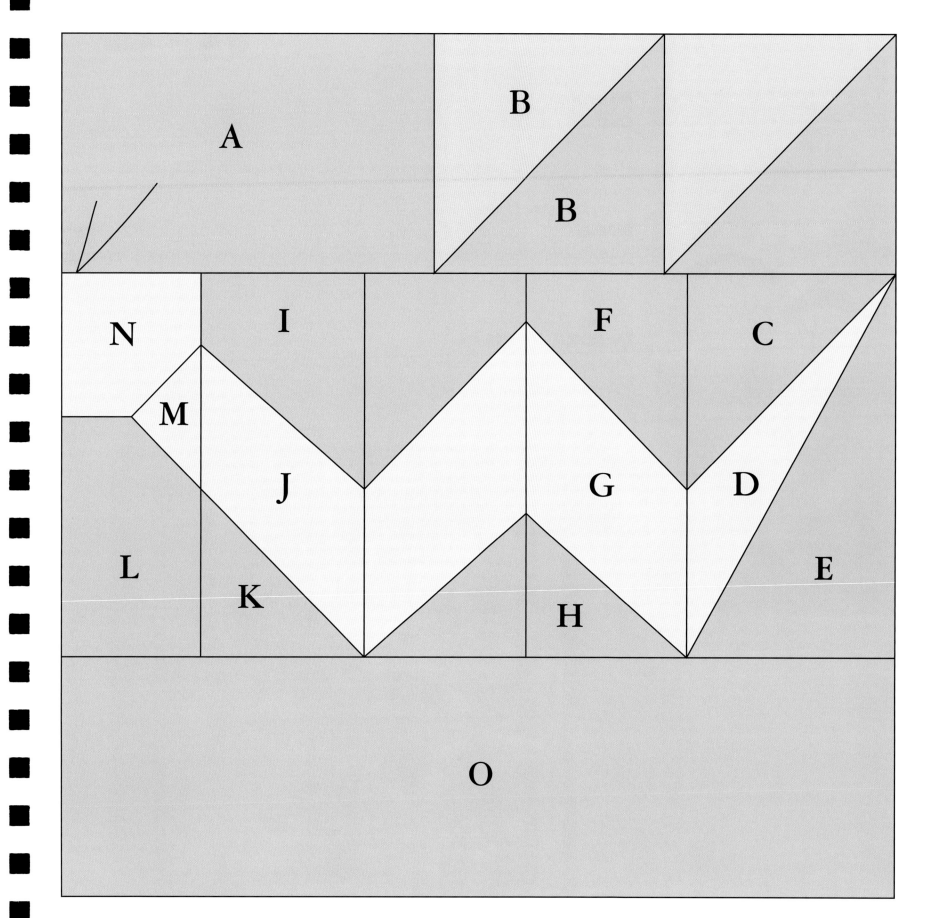

Johnny-Jump-Ups

BLOCK

Cut

Background: Cut 1. All other pieces: Fuse double-sided webbing to fabrics. Leaves: Cut 2. Large petals: Cut 3. Small petals: Cut 6. Butterfly: Cut 1. (Do not add seam allowances to fused pieces.)

Stitch

Place and fuse all pieces. By machine, appliqué all fused pieces using narrow zigzag stitch. Use same stitch to make flower stalks and butterfly antennae. Sew buttons in middle of flowers, and sew beads to middle of butterfly and to end of antennae.

QUILTED FLOWERS

Make 4 blocks. Stitch together as shown, adding sashing. Add rickrack border (see page 183). Finished size is about 28 inches square.

Fluttering by Butterfly

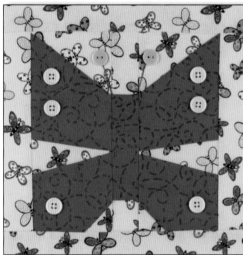

BLOCK

Cut

A–E: Cut 1 each, and cut 1 each from reverse pattern. F–H: Cut 1 each. I: Cut 2. J: Cut 2.

Stitch

Stitch A to B, stitch C to other side of B; stitch D to other side of C, and then stitch E to inside corner of D (wing piece). Make 2 (1 is reverse pattern). Stitch F to G, and stitch H to other side of G. Stitch wing piece to FGH, and then stitch reverse wing piece to other side of FGH. Stitch an I to either side of square, and then stitch a J to top and bottom to complete block. By machine, use narrow zigzag stitch to make antennae. Sew buttons to tops of antennae and along sides of wings.

A BOUNTY OF BUTTERFLIES

Make 27 blocks. Cut 36 fabric squares, and add I and J pieces to sides to make 9-inch squares. Sew them together as shown. Add border. Finished size is about 67×85 inches.

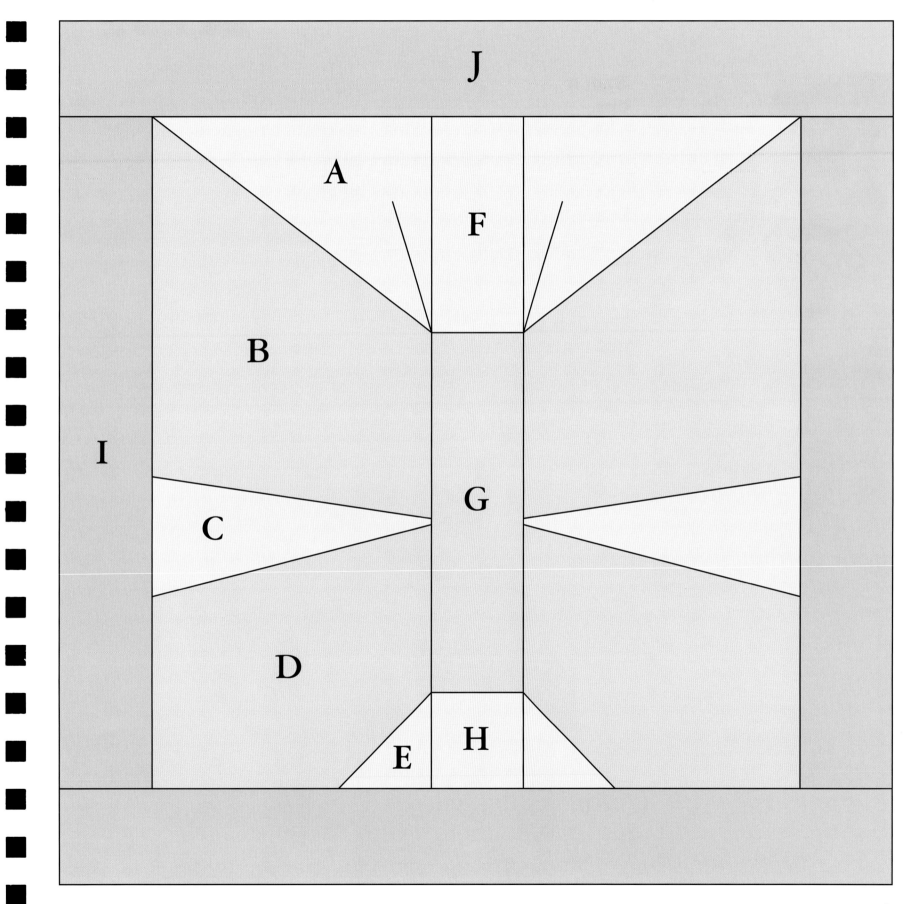

Gossamer Wings

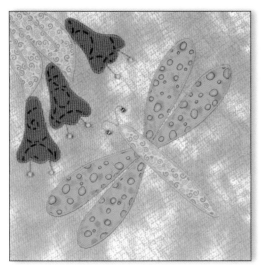

BLOCK

Cut

Background: Cut 1. All other pieces: Fuse double-sided webbing to fabrics. Body: Cut 1. Wings: Cut 4. Flowers: Cut 3. Leaves: Cut 1 each. (Do not add seam allowances to fused pieces.)

Stitch

Place and fuse all pieces. By machine, appliqué all fused pieces using narrow zigzag stitch. Use same stitch to make flower stamen, leaf veins, and dragonfly antennae. Sew beads to ends of stamen and antennae.

WINGED CHAIR PILLOW

Make 1 block, and add borders to fit size of pillow form. Add long ties to attach pillow to chair or stool. Finished size depends on size of pillow form.

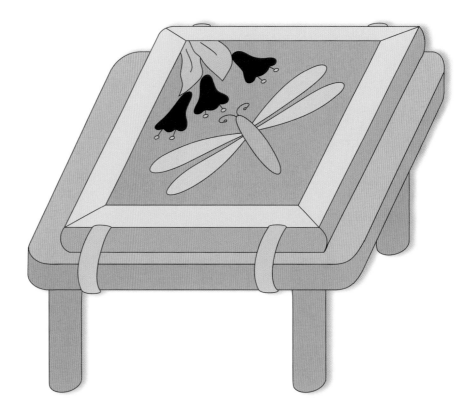

Garden Queen Iris

BLOCK

Cut

Background: Cut 1. All other pieces: Fuse double-sided webbing to fabrics. Leaves: Cut 1 each. Upper petals: Cut 2, and cut 2 from reverse pattern. Lower petals: Cut 2, and cut 2 from reverse pattern. (Do not add seam allowances to fused pieces.)

Stitch

Place and fuse all pieces. By machine, appliqué all fused pieces using narrow zigzag stitch. Use same stitch to make flower stalks. (Option: Hand-stitch cording to background for flower stems.) Sew a button to middle of each flower.

HANDBAG FIT FOR A QUEEN

Make 1 block, and sew to bag. Add diamond star squares border (see page 190) to each side of bag. Finished size depends on size of bag.

Good Morning Glory

BLOCK
Cut
Background: Cut 1. All other pieces: Fuse double-sided webbing to fabrics. Flower centers, flowers, leaves: Cut 3 each. (Do not add seam allowances to fused pieces.)

Stitch
Place and fuse all pieces. By machine, appliqué all fused pieces using narrow zigzag stitch. Use same stitch to make flower vines, leaf veins, and tendrils.

MORNING GLORY CHAIR PADS
Make 1 block, and add top and side borders to fit chair back. Use quilt batting between pad face and back. Add ties to attach pad to chair. Finished size depends on chair size.

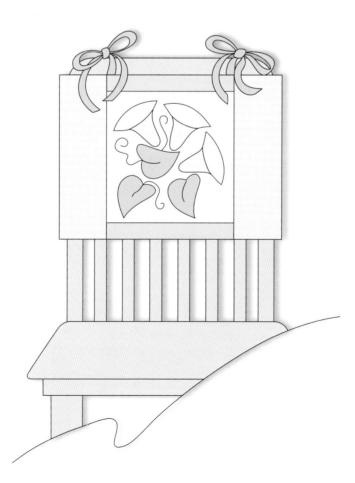

Bloom Well Groomed

BLOCK

Cut

Background: Cut 1. All other pieces: Fuse double-sided webbing to fabrics, and cut 1 each. (Do not add seam allowances to fused pieces.)

Stitch

Place and fuse all pieces. By machine, appliqué all fused pieces using narrow zigzag stitch. Use same stitch to make flower stamen. Sew buttons to ends of stamen. Hand-stitch green cord on background for flower stem.

QUILT A BLOOM

Make 32 blocks, and cut 32 fabric squares. Stitch them together as shown, adding sashing. Sew on double border. Finished size is about 87 inches square.

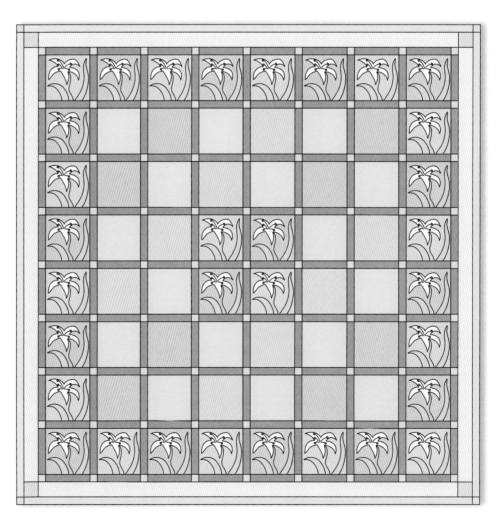

Birdhouse Treasure

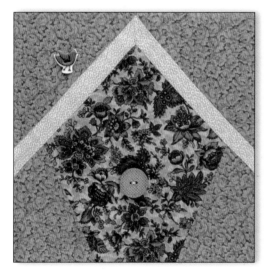

BLOCK
Cut

A–C: Cut 1, and cut 1 from reverse pattern. D: Cut 1.

Stitch

Stitch A to B; make 2 (1 is reverse pattern). Stitch AB to reverse AB at narrow end. Stitch C to D, and stitch reverse C to other side of D. Stitch ABBA to top of CDC. Sew a large button to D for birdhouse hole, and sew on a decorative bird button, if desired.

BIRD HOUSE HANGING

Make 3 blocks, and add block leaf border (see page 176) around each block. Stitch blocks in a row. Add loops for hanging. Finished size is about 39×13 inches.

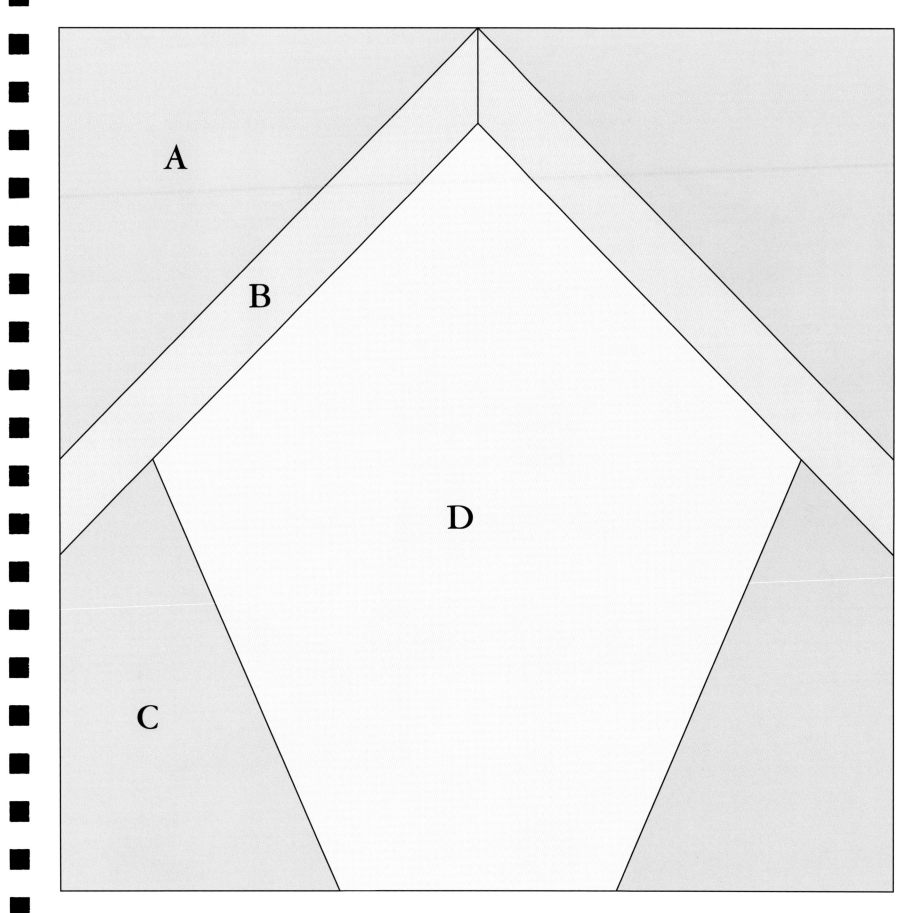

A

B

C

D

Pretty Bird

BLOCK

Cut

A: Cut 2. B–J: Cut 1 each.

Stitch

Stitch C to B, and stitch D to BC. Stitch A to BCD, and stitch A to other side of BCD. Stitch E to F, then stitch G to EF. Stitch H to other side of EFG. Stitch I to EFGH. Stitch J to bottom of EFGHI. Stitch 2 pieces together to complete block. Sew a bead on for eye.

PRETTY PILLOW

Make 1 block, and add border. Finished size is about 14 inches square.

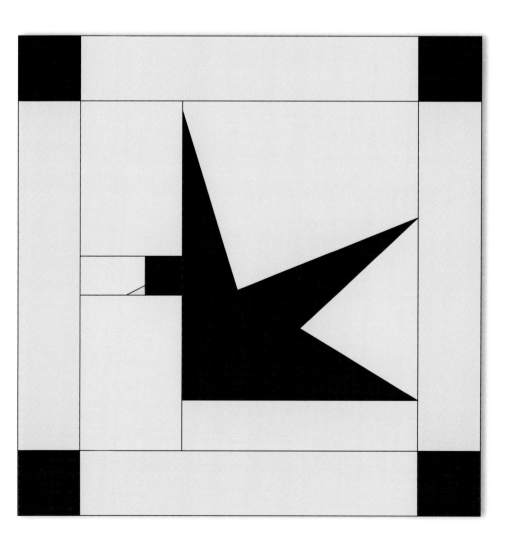

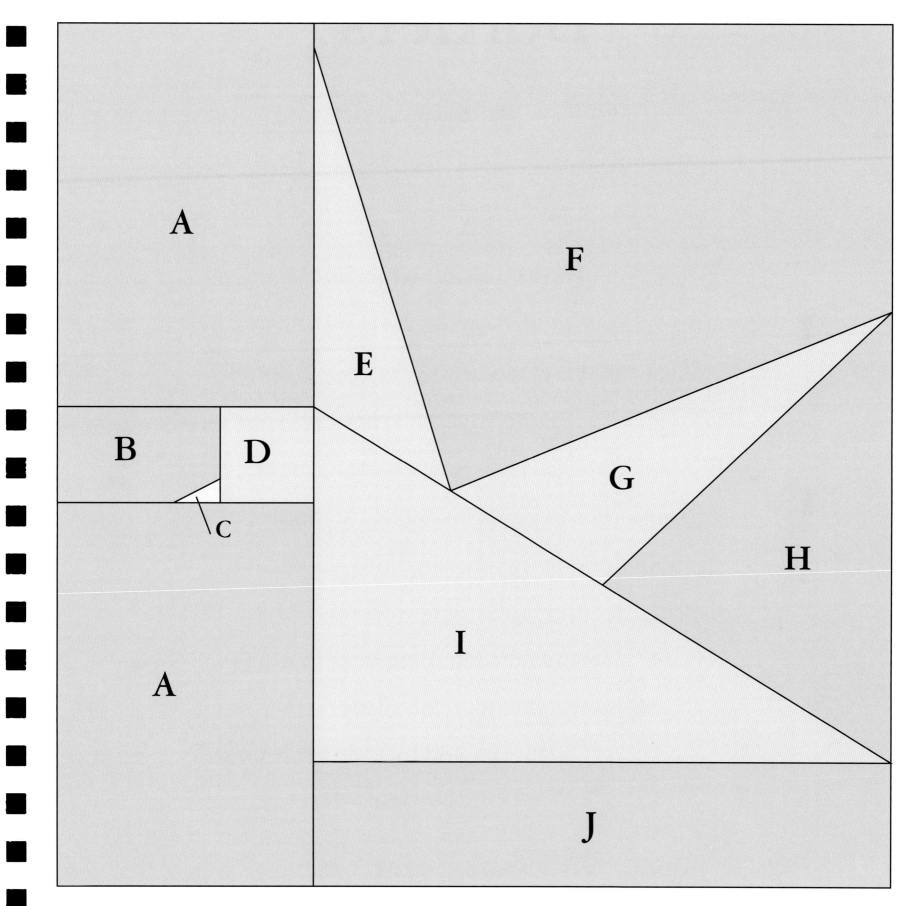

Borders

◆◗◆◗◆

You've spent weeks, months, maybe even years completing your quilt. Now what? How will you best display all the wonderful work you've done? Add a spectacular border that will show off your quilt! The borders in this chapter range from a simple picture frame border to a patchwork bricks border to a more difficult but dazzling braided border. With 20 different borders to choose from, you're sure to find something here that will showcase the quilt you made with such care and love.

Block Leaf

Make Border

Sew an A to both sides of B to create block. Sew blocks together to needed lengths, alternating leaf angles to create pattern.

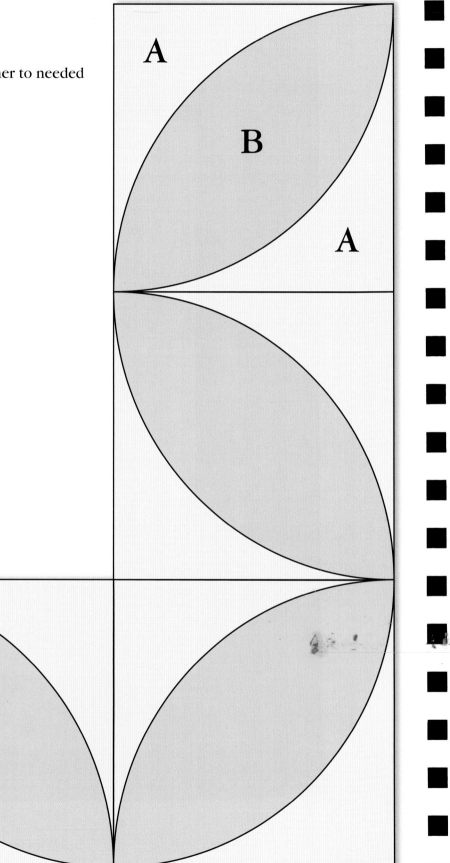

Rambling Leaves

Make Border

Cut border strips to needed lengths, and miter corners. Fuse double-sided fusible webbing to fabric for leaves, and cut out enough leaves for 1 leaf every 3 inches, with 2 leaves at each corner. Fuse leaves to border strips. By machine, appliqué all fused pieces using narrow zigzag stitch. Make a vine with same stitch.

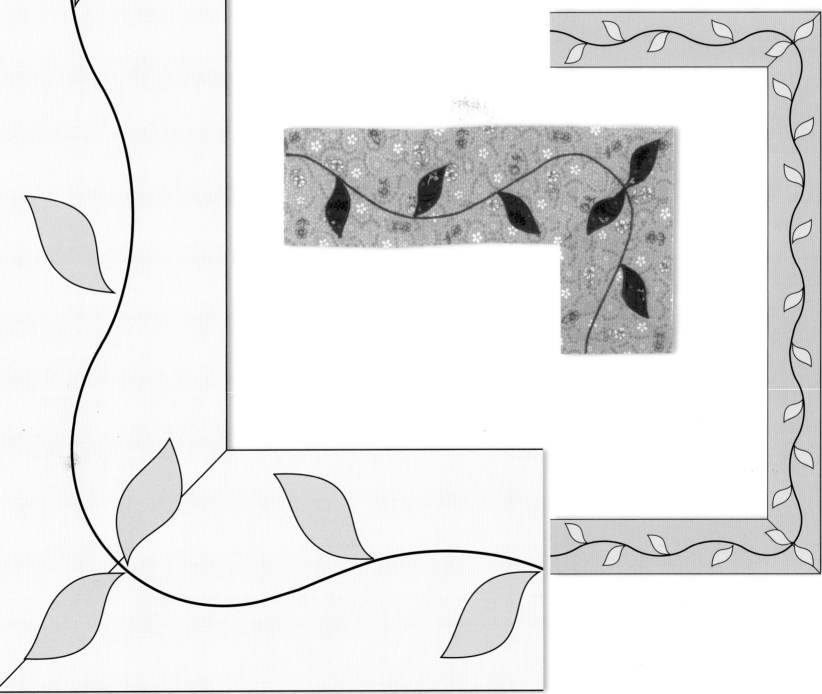

Double Picture Frame

Make Border

Cut inner and outer border strips to needed lengths.

Miter corners.

Flowers and More

Make Border

Cut border strips to needed lengths, and miter corners. Cut off triangle at corners. Iron double-sided fusible webbing to flower and stem/leaf fabrics. Cut out flowers, stems, and leaves from fabric; fuse to border strips. By machine, appliqué all fused pieces using narrow zigzag stitch.

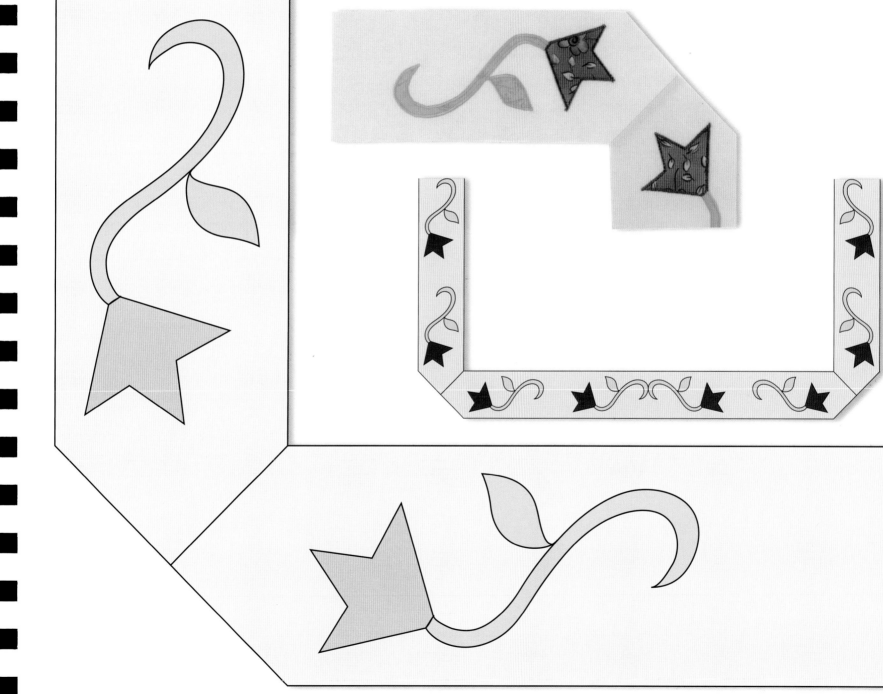

Blocks and Bars

Make Border

Sew A to contrasting A. Sew B blocks to either side of AA's, repeating to make border strips to needed lengths. Adjust length of A's to fit quilt.

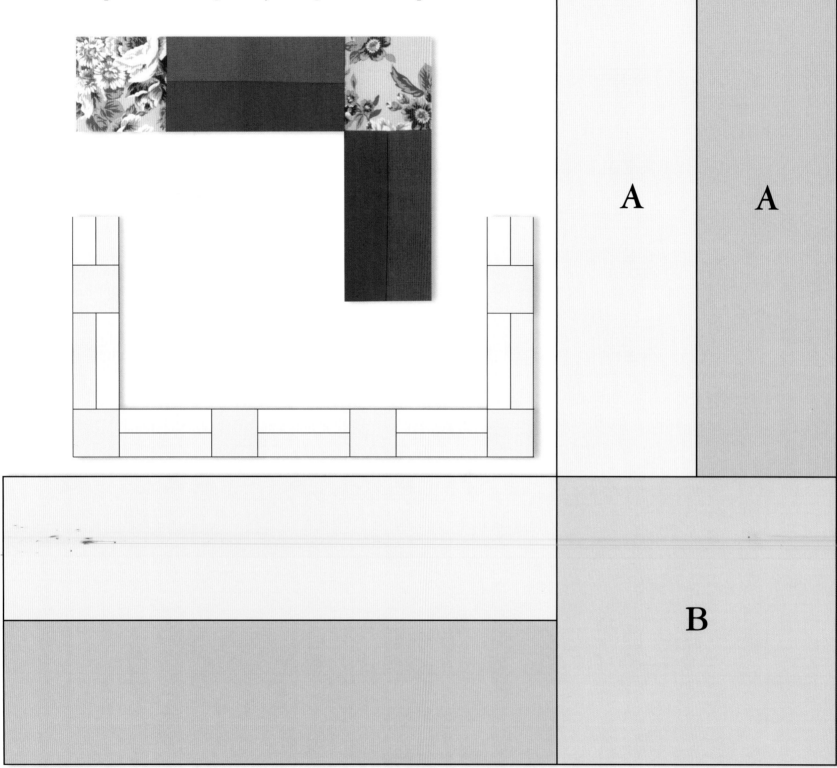

Make Border

Cut fabrics into strips. Cut rectangles (3½, 4½, and 5½ inches long) from fabrics, and sew rectangles into strips. Sew strips together to create a double border to needed lengths. (Seam allowances were added to measurements.)

Piano Keys

Make Border

Corner square: Sew A to A, then stitch B to side of AA. Stitch on C, then D. Stitch on E, then F. Sides: Stitch F's together to needed lengths.

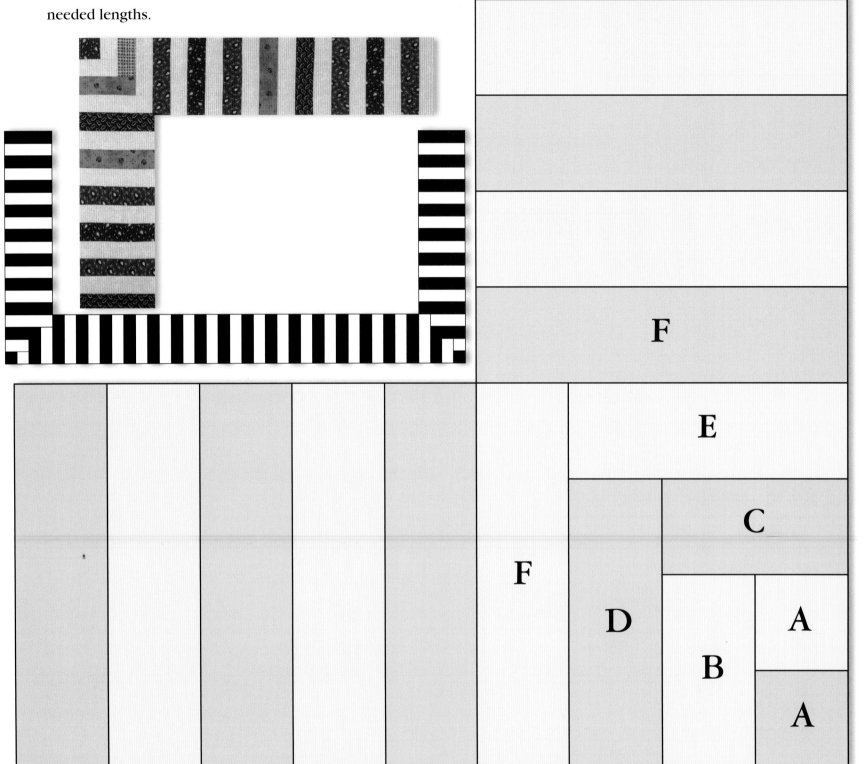

Make Border

Corner square: Sew A to B; stitch C to AB. Stitch D to BAC, and stitch E to DBAC. Sides: Cut middle strips and inner and outer strips to needed lengths. Sew narrow strips to either side of wider strip. Sew strips and corners together, and stitch rickrack to inner and outer strips.

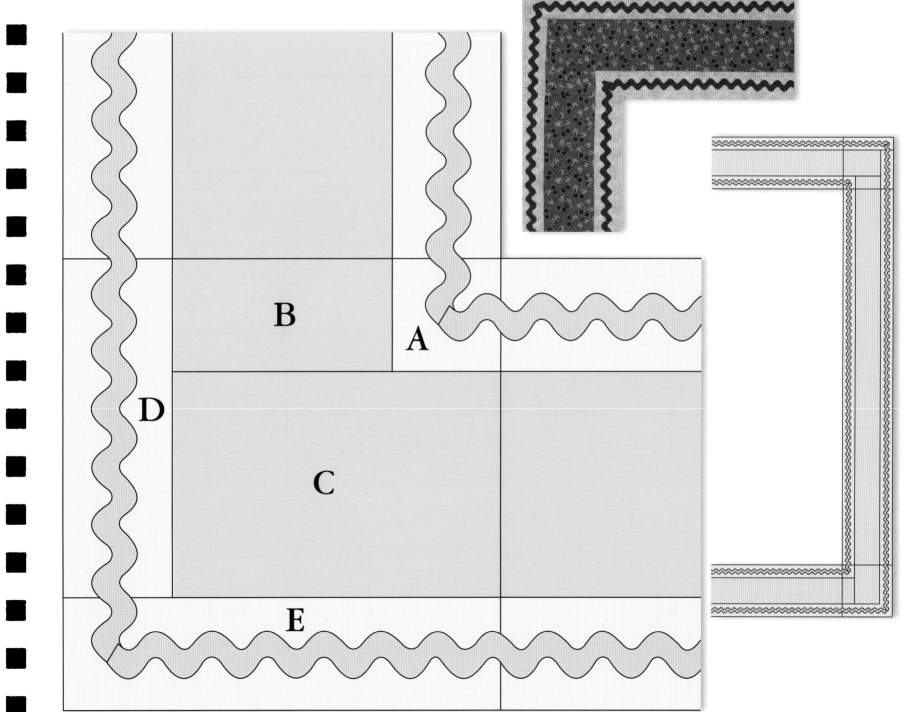

Flying Geese

Make Border

Stitch triangle to contrasting triangle. Sew blocks together to needed lengths, matching unlike fabrics. For center of each side, stitch a block of matching fabrics to create larger triangle.

Scalloped

Make Border

Make a template for scallop, adjusting space between points to make strips needed lengths. Trace template onto fabric, cutting 2 strips per side. Miter corners, and stitch strips right sides together. Clip curves, turn, and iron flat.

Stop Sign

Make Border

Sew A's to short sides of B to create a square. Stitch squares together to needed lengths.

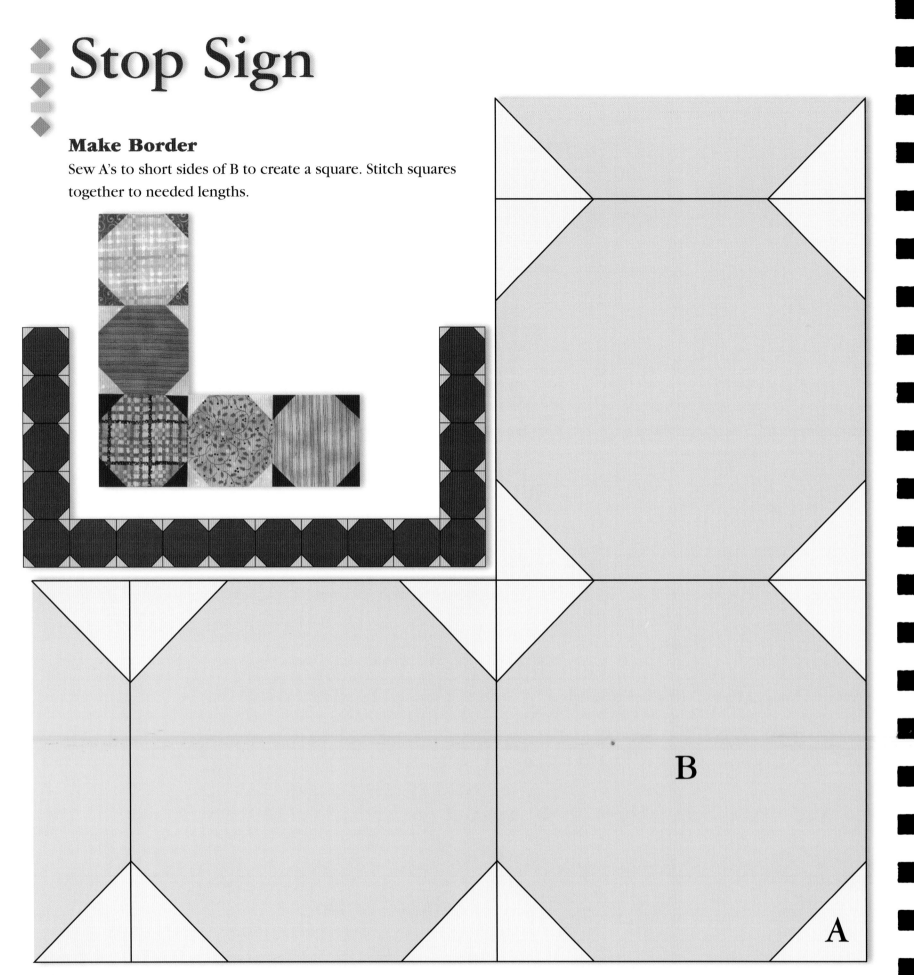

Make Border

Cut strips to needed lengths; stitch strips together. Use bias tape or make bias strips with a bias tape maker. Stitch bias strip around border, creating a wavy line. Sew right sides of hearts to fusible side of webbing; stitch, clip curves, and trim seam allowances. Make a small cut in webbing, and turn. Fuse hearts to sides of bias tape. At corners, fuse 4 hearts point to point to create a flower. By hand or machine, appliqué all hearts using narrow blanket stitch.

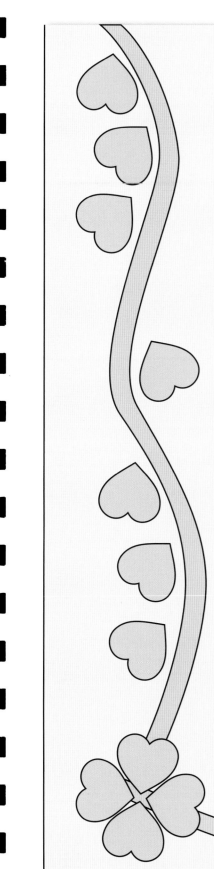

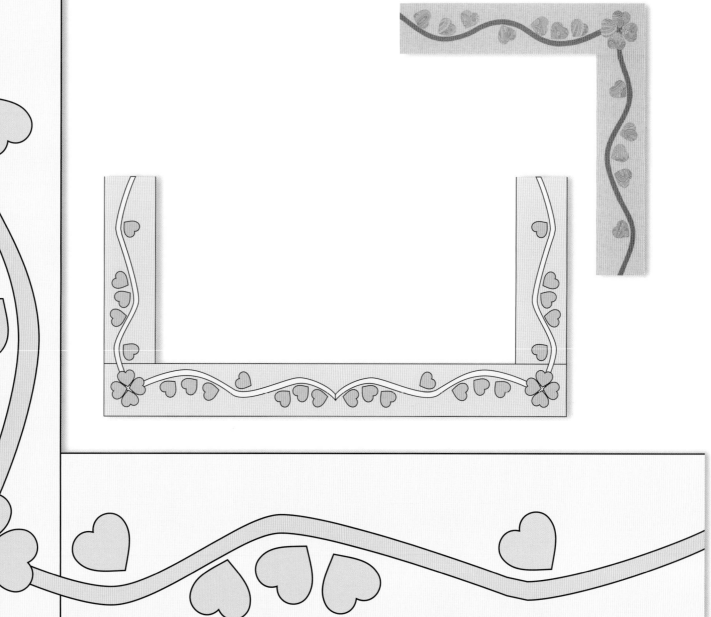

Churn Dash

Make Border

Follow instructions for center of churn dash block (see page 68), using only pieces A, B, and C. Cut three 1½-inch-wide strips (seam allowances are added to measurement) from 2 different fabrics; sew strips together with darkest fabric inside. Measure and cut strips; space blocks evenly between strips.

A A B B C

Bars and Blocks

Make Border

Cut A's and B's from fabric and contrast fabric. Stitch A to contrast A to A. Stitch contrast B to B to contrast B. Stitch AAA's to BBB's to create needed lengths. For each corner, stitch a 9-patch with B's, using 5 B's and 4 contrast B's.

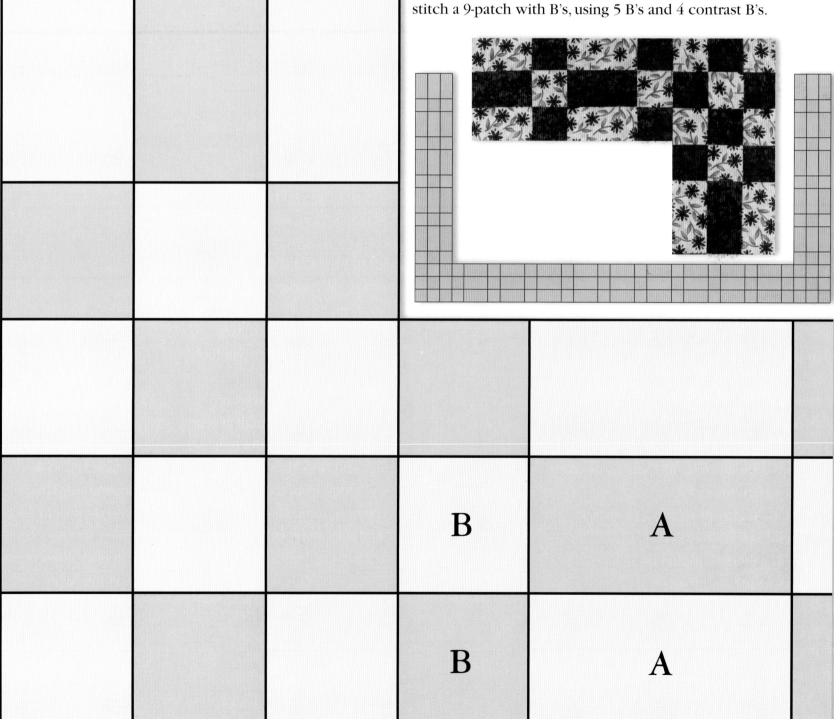

B   **A**

B   **A**

Diamond Star Squares

Make Border

Sew A's to sides of B's to create strips to needed lengths. At corners, stitch C's to fit smaller spaces. Cut inner and outer strips of contrasting fabric, miter corners, and stitch to squares strip.

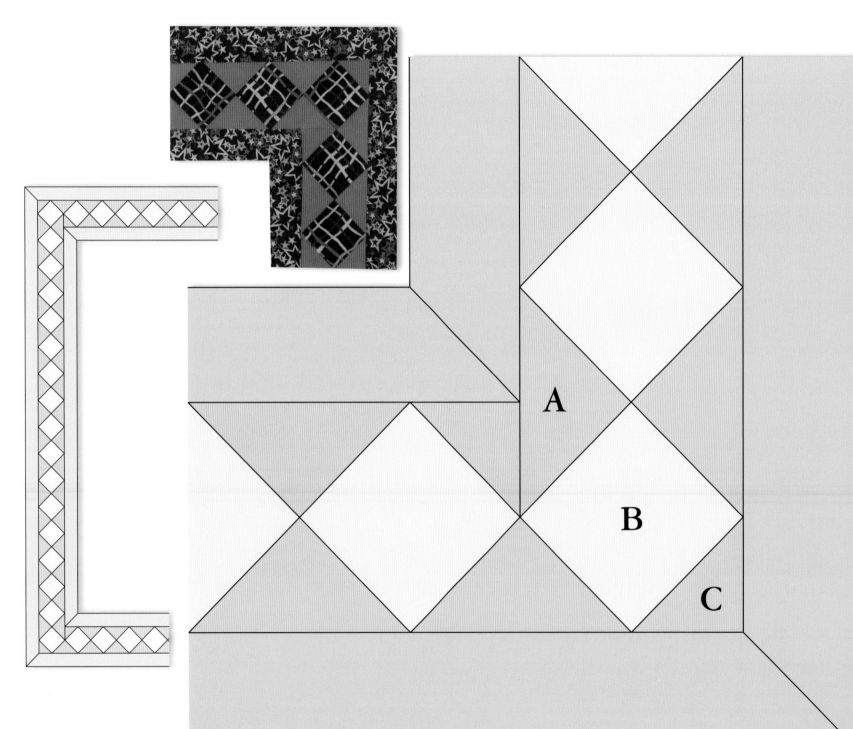

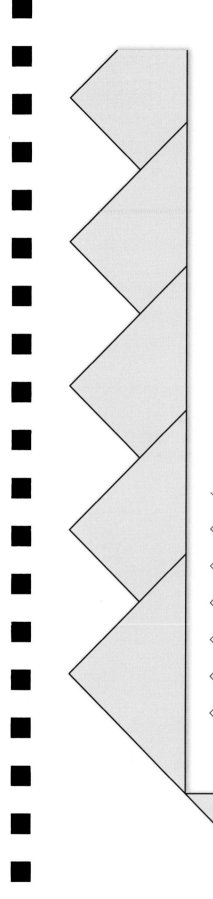

Make Border

STEP 1: Cut 3-inch strips to needed lengths. Fold strip in half, and iron to crease. Open. From bottom edge to crease, make a vertical cut every 3 inches. From top to crease, cut off 1½ inches from right side of fabric. Make a vertical cut every 3 inches down to crease.

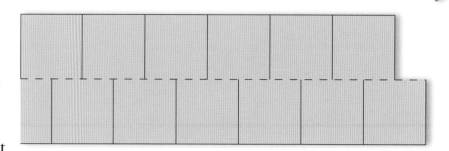

STEP 2: Work with wrong side of fabric up. Above crease, fold down top left corner of each square to crease to make triangles. Below crease, fold up bottom left corner to crease to make triangles. Iron.

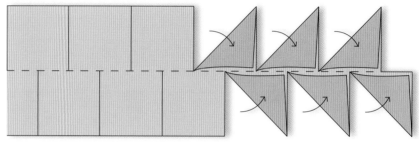

STEP 3: Fold bottom up at crease. Fold triangles in back row to front, and fold triangles in front to back. Baste along bottom edge.

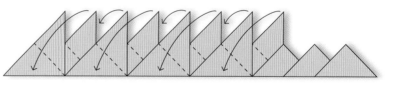

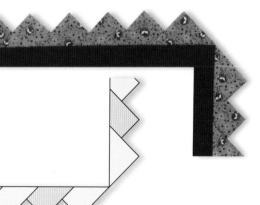

Sawtooth Square

Make Border

Stitch A to contrast A. Stitch AA to B, then stitch another AA to other side. Stitch AA to contrast B, then stitch another AA to other side. Stitch AABAA's together to needed lengths. Stitch a 9-patch made with B's to corners.

Braided

Make Border

Cut strips from light and dark fabrics. Stitch strip 1 to the end of strip 2, creating a 90-degree angle. Stitch strip 3 to strip 2 and its end to strip 1. Stitch 4 to 1 and its end to 3. Continue adding strips to needed lengths. Stitch triangles made with strips to corners. So all corners are symmetrical, stitch a square in middle of sides. Baste along both edges of border before sewing to quilt top and binding.

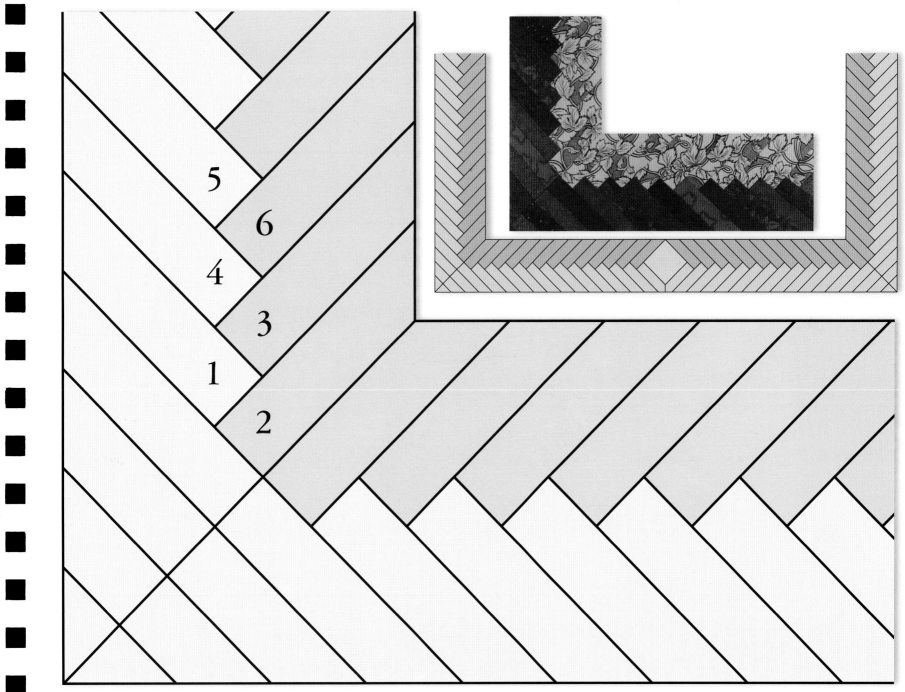

Eight-Pointed Star

Make Border

Stitch contrast A to second contrast A; make 4. Stitch AA blocks together to make pinwheel. Stitch background A to contrast A's; make 8. Stitch contrast AA to second contrast AA, matching background A's; make 4. Stitch B to AAAA, and stitch B to other side. Make 2. Stitch pieces together to complete block. Make number of blocks needed for lengths. Set star squares on point, and sew D's to sides of stars to make strips. Sew C's at corners to fill in smaller spaces.

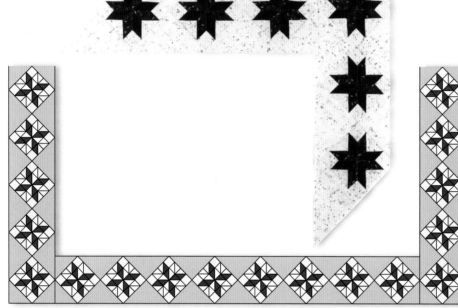

Make Border

Sew B to A, then sew B to other side of A. Stitch rectangles together to needed lengths. Sew C to corner. Cut inner and outer strips to needed lengths, and stitch to triangles strip.

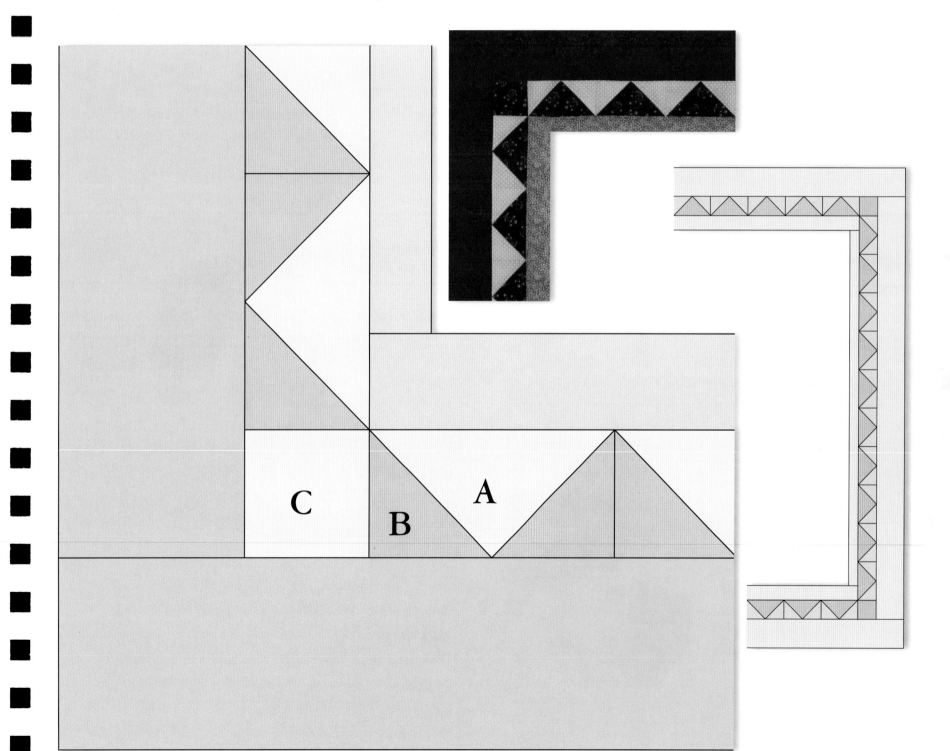

Start a Quilting Adventure!

People have been making quilts for centuries. With today's time-saving techniques, even the busiest person can express love by making a quilt. There is no greater gift than something you've made by hand—the receiver knows it comes straight from the heart!

So set aside the household chores, and indulge yourself. Use the timeless craft of quilting to create family treasures.

MATERIALS

Fabric

Invest in the best materials you can afford. Many inexpensive fabrics are less likely to be colorfast. Avoid the regret that goes with choosing a fabric that isn't quite perfect because it is less expensive than the fabric you love.

Select 100 percent cotton fabrics for the face and back. Cotton is easy to cut, mark, sew, and press. It is also widely available. Fabrics that contain synthetics, such as polyester, are more difficult to handle and more likely to pucker.

Make quilts any color scheme that appeals to you. In general, select colors of one type—such as brights or pastels—to use in one quilt. Use cool colors such as purple, blue, and white or warm colors such as yellow, orange, red, and cream.

Sometimes a fabric that seems light by itself is very dark next to other fabrics. To avoid this, look at all the fabrics you plan to use through a red transparent report cover (available in most stationery stores). Do the fabrics you thought were dark look dark next to the ones you thought were light? Do you have fabrics of all values? Do the values create the effect you are trying to achieve?

Use prints with a variety of scales or all with similar scales. That is, use large prints, medium prints, and small prints in the same quilt or use only large, medium, or small prints. If you use all small prints with one large print, the large print will look out of place.

When you have selected the fabrics, buy a small amount of each (¼ yard). Make one block, and then evaluate it. Are you happy with all the fabrics and how they work together? Step back, and look at the block from a distance. Does it still look good? This is the time to make changes, but be sure you do it right away so the fabric is still available.

The backing fabric should be similar in fiber content and care to the fabrics used for the quilt top. Some wide cottons (90 and 108 inches) are sold for quilt backings.

Batting

There are many types of batting. In general, use polyester batting with low or medium loft. For a puffier quilt, use high loft, but it is difficult to quilt. If you use this batting, consider tying instead of quilting. Polyester batting is best if the quilt will be washed frequently. Cotton batting is preferred by some quilters for a flat, traditional look. Wool batting is a pleasure to quilt and makes a warm cover.

Thread

It may seem tempting to use up old thread on a quilt. However, working with old, weak thread is frustrating because it tangles and knots. Consider buying 100 percent cotton thread or good long-staple polyester thread for piecing, appliqué, and machine quilting. Use monofilament nylon thread (.004mm or size 80) for freehand machine quilting. Cotton quilting thread is wonderful for hand quilting but should not be used for machine quilting because it is stiff and will tend to lay on the surface of the quilt.

For piecing by hand or by machine, select a neutral color that blends with most of the fabrics in the quilt. Use white thread for basting; colored thread may leave color behind on the fabric. For appliqué, the thread should match the fabric that is being applied to the background. The color of quilting thread is a personal design choice. If you want your quilting to show up, use a contrasting thread color.

TOOL SELECTION

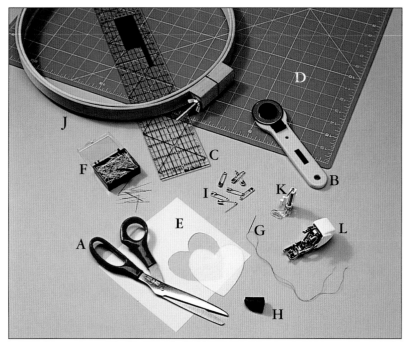

A sharp pair of scissors (A) is essential for quilting. Ideally, set aside a pair of scissors to be used only on fabric. Paper and plastic quickly dull the cutting edges of scissors, so keep a separate pair of scissors for cutting out templates and other nonfabric uses.

To cut fabric quickly and easily, invest in a rotary cutter (B), see-through ruler (C), and self-healing mat (D). These tools help you cut strips of fabric efficiently. If you become very involved with quilting, you may find that a collection of cutters, mats, and rulers of different sizes and shapes is valuable. A good starter set would include a large cutter, a mat at least 22 inches wide, and a 6×24-inch ruler.

Most fabrics can be marked with a hard lead pencil. Mechanical pencils are worthwhile investments because they are always sharp. A special eraser can help remove light pencil markings. Other handy marking tools include colored pencils designed for marking on fabric and a fine-tip permanent pen for signing your finished quilt. Soapstone pencils make a light mark that is easy to brush off, but they lose their sharp point quickly and must be sharpened often. Tailor's chalk or chalk wheels are helpful for marking quilting patterns just before you quilt. The chalk brushes off fabric easily. Disappearing ink pens may be tempting because they make a mark that is easy to see, but heating fabric (such as by ironing) that contains ink residue can create a permanent stain. Leaving a work in progress in a hot car or in a sunny window can also cause this to happen. Consider banning this product from your quilting basket.

Traditionally, templates were made of scrap cardboard. Cardboard is fine, but if a template is going to be used many times, template plastic is better because it does not wear down. Template plastic (E) is available as plain white sheets or transparent sheets printed with a grid.

For some projects, freezer paper (plastic-coated paper sold in supermarkets) is useful. It is often used in appliqué.

The shape to be appliquéd is cut out of freezer paper without seam allowances. Place the shiny side against the right side of the fabric, and iron it to the fabric. Cut the shape out, adding a ³⁄₁₆-inch seam allowance. As you stitch the piece to the background, turn under the seam allowance to the edge of the paper. Peel off the paper after stitching.

The pins used for hand piecing and hand appliqué are called sharps (F). For hand quilting, the needles are called betweens (G). As a beginner, you should start using a size 8 and work toward using a size 10 or 12. Use the smallest needle you can to make the smallest stitches. A quilter's thimble (H) will protect your finger.

Always use a sharp needle on your sewing machine; a dull needle will tend to skip stitches and snag the threads of your fabric, creating puckers. Use size 9/70 or 11/80 for piecing and appliqué and size 11/80 (in most cases) or 14/90 (for a thick quilt) for machine quilting.

Use fine, sharp straight pins (such as silk pins) for piecing and holding appliqué pieces in place before basting or stitching. Long quilter's pons are used to hold the layers (top, batting, and backing) before they are basted together or quilted. Have a large box of size 2 safety pins (I) on hand for basting and for machine quilting.

If you plan to quilt by hand, you need some way of holding the area you are stitching smooth. Some people do this successfully with their hands, but most quilters prefer to use a quilting hoop (J) or quilting frame. Quilting hoops are portable and inexpensive. A small area of the quilt is surrounded by the hoop, which keeps the fabric taut. For large bed quilts, many quilters prefer to use a quilting frame, which supports the entire quilt and displays large areas for quilting. However, quilt frames are a significant investment and require space. Consider using quilt hoops until you feel the need to work on a quilt frame. Experiment with different tools to see what feels most comfortable.

You will need a steam iron and ironing board. For streamlining your work, place the ironing board at right angles to the sewing table and raise it to the same height. This will allow you to press seams after they are stitched.

Quilts can be made by hand. Today, however, many quilters do all piecing and some do all quilting by machine. The machine does not have to make many fancy stitches. It does need to stitch an accurate ¼-inch seam with an even tension, though. A darning foot (K) and an even-feed walking foot (L) are necessary machine attachments.

MATERIAL PREPARATION

Prewashing

Always wash fabrics first. This will remove some of the chemicals added by the manufacturer, making it easier to quilt. Also, cotton fabric does shrink, and most of the shrinkage will occur during the first washing and drying. Be sure to use settings that are as hot as those you intend to use when you wash the finished quilt.

Dark, intense colors, especially reds, tend to bleed or run. Wash these fabrics by themselves. If the water becomes colored, try soaking the fabric in a solution of three parts cold water to one part white wine vinegar. Rinse thoroughly. Wash again. If the fabric is still losing color, discard the fabric and select another. It is not worth using a fabric that may ruin the other fabrics when the finished quilt is washed.

Making Templates

To make templates from full-size patterns, trace the pattern onto template plastic with a sharp pencil or a fine-tip permanent pen. Use scissors to cut out the templates.

Marking and Cutting Fabric

To cut fabric the traditional way for piecing or appliqué, place the template on the wrong side of the fabric. The arrow on the template indicating the grain should be aligned with the straight grain or the crosswise grain of the fabric.

Trace around the template with a hard lead pencil or a colored pencil designed for marking on fabric. Yellow or silver pencils, for example, show up well on dark fabrics. Never use a ballpoint pen or other marking tool that has ink that may run. If the template does not include a seam allowance, add one. Cut around each piece with sharp fabric scissors.

In many cases, it is faster and easier to cut fabric using a rotary cutter. This tool, which looks and works like a pizza cutter, must be used with a self-healing mat and a see-through ruler. (Always put the safety shield of the rotary cutter in place when it is not in use.)

Fold the fabric in half lengthwise with the selvages together. Adjust one side until the fabric hangs straight. The line created by the fold is parallel to the fabric's straight of grain. Keeping this fold in place, lay the fabric on the mat.

Place a see-through ruler on the fabric. Align a grid line on the ruler with the fold and trim the uneven edge. Apply steady, even pressure to the rotary cutter and to the ruler to keep them and the fabric from shifting. Do not let the cutter get farther away from

you than your hand holding the ruler. Stop cutting, and reposition your hand.

Reposition the ruler so that it covers the width of the strip to be cut and the trimmed edge is on the marking for the appropriate measurement on the ruler.

After cutting the strip, hold it up to make sure it is straight. If it is angled, refold the fabric and trim it again. Continue cutting strips, checking frequently that the strips are straight.

PATCHWORK TECHNIQUES

Unless otherwise noted, add ¼-inch seam allowances for all patterns in this book. Measurements given are of finished pieces; they do not have seam allowances added—you will need to add them.

Accuracy is important. A small error repeated in each block or, worse yet, in each seam, will become a large distortion. Before starting a large project, make a sample block and measure it. Is it the desired size? If not, figure out where the inaccuracy occurred. Are any seams a few threads too wide or narrow? Clip seams, and restitch.

Hand Piecing

With right sides together, align fabric pattern pieces so that the fabric ends match.

(Use straight pins to check.) Pin the seam. Make sure the fabric edges match exactly.

Cut a piece of thread approximately 18 inches long. Put the end that came off the spool of thread first through the eye of the needle. Knot the other end of the thread, using a quilter's knot.

To make a quilter's knot, wrap the end of the thread around the tip of the needle (wrapping from the base toward the point of the needle) three times. Then pull the needle through the wraps. Pull the knot down to the end.

Stitch from one end of the seam to the other, using a

running stitch (about eight stitches per inch). For added strength, back-stitch at the beginning and end of each seam. Do not stitch across the seam allowance. In general, press the seam toward the darker fabric.

Machine Piecing

When piecing using a machine, set the sewing machine's stitch length to 10 to 12 stitches per inch (or between 2 and 3 on machines that do not use stitches per inch). Stitch across the seam allowance, along the seam line, and

across the seam allowance at the far end of the seam. Do not backstitch.

Make sure the seam allowance is consistently ¼ inch. The presser foot on a few sewing machines is a true ¼ inch. Stitch a sample, and measure the seam allowance. If you are off by just a hair on each piece you stitch, the errors will accumulate and the end result may be a distorted block.

If your machine does not have a mark or a ¼-inch-wide presser foot, place masking tape on the plate under the presser foot to act as a sewing guide. Make a sample, and measure it for accuracy.

Piecing Curves

Fold each curved piece in half to find the center of the seam. Clip the concave curve ³⁄₁₆-inch deep approximately every ½ inch along a tight curve (cut less often for a gradual curve). With the two pieces right sides together, match the center of each seam and the end points. Pin. With the concave curve on top, stitch slowly, easing the fabric so the edges stay even.

Chain Piecing for Efficiency

To streamline the sewing of multiple units, use chain piecing. Stitch a seam, and then without removing that unit from the sewing

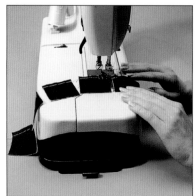

machine, insert the next unit. Continue stitching from one unit to the next. Make as many units as practical in one long chain. Then snip the connecting threads, and press each unit. During the course of a project this technique can save a substantial amount of time.

Strip Piecing

Strip piecing is another technique that can save a lot of time. Instead of using templates, cut strips of fabric. (Use a rotary cutter and a ruler for the greatest efficiency.) Stitch the strips of fabric together. Then cut

those strips, and recombine the resulting units.

Paper Piecing

Paper piecing involves stitching pieces of fabric together on a paper foundation. This foundation stabilizes the fabric, keeping it from stretching and shifting. This is helpful when working with unusual fabrics such as those used in crazy quilts. If the stitching lines are drawn on the foundation papers, this technique can also produce extremely accurate piecing.

Hand Appliqué

Prepare pieces of fabric to be appliquéd by hand by tracing around the template on the right side of the fabric. Add a ³⁄₁₆-inch seam allowance as you cut out each piece. Fold under the seam allowance along the marked seam line. Baste around each piece to hold the seam allowances under, clipping where necessary.

Pin the first piece to be stitched to the background. Hand-stitch it to the background with a blind stitch or, for a more decorative look, use a blanket stitch and contrasting thread.

When the appliqué is complete, consider carefully trimming the background fabric from behind the appliqué inside the stitching line. This must be done with great care so that the appliqué is not snipped, but it does reduce the bulk and makes it easier to quilt.

Machine Appliqué

For machine appliqué, there is no seam allowance added to each pattern piece. Instead, simply cut around the template. Use fusible webbing to hold the pattern piece firmly in place. Follow the manufacturer's instructions to bond the webbing to the back of the pattern piece, remove the protective paper, and then bond the pattern piece to the

background fabric. Stitch around the piece using an ¹⁄₈-inch-wide to ³⁄₁₆-inch-wide zigzag stitch or narrow blanket stitch. The stitches should be close together but not so close that the fabric does not feed smoothly through the machine.

FINISHING TOUCHES
Assembling the Quilt Top

Arrange the completed quilt blocks. Sew the blocks together to form rows. Press. Sew the rows together.

Pressing

Press completed quilt blocks from the back first and then lightly from the front. Do not apply pressure because this may stretch and distort the fabric. Instead, rely on lots of steam to do the work.

Press the completed quilt top before basting it to the batting and backing. Do not press a quilt once the batting has been added because this will flatten it.

Adding Borders

Add borders that are not pieced by sewing strips of fabric (of the desired width) to the long sides of the quilt. Trim the ends of the strips even with the short sides of the quilt. Then, stitch strips of fabric to the short sides, stitching across the borders previously applied.

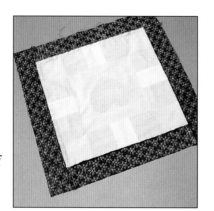

Press the borders and the seam allowances away from the center of the quilt. If there is more than one border, stitch on the borders in the same order for each border.

In some quilts, mitered corners, which require a little more time and care, look better than square or butted cor-

ners. Find the center of each border strip and the center of each side of the quilt. One side at a time, pin the border and stitch, beginning and ending ¼ inch from the edge of the quilt top. (Borders need strips longer than the sides for mitering.)

With right sides together, fold the quilt top diagonally, matching seams and the edges of the borders. Use a ruler and pencil to extend across the border strips to the line formed by the fold.

Taking care not to snag the seam allowances, stitch from the inside edge of the border to the outer corner on the marked line. Trim the ends of the border strips, and press the seam open. Repeat for each corner.

Finishing the Outer Edges

Decide how you will finish the outer edges of your quilt before you prepare for quilting. Traditionally, the outer edges of a quilt are encased in binding after the quilt is quilted. The binding wears better than other options so the time spent applying the binding is worth it if you want the quilt to last a long time. Binding techniques are described on page 205.

A faster technique, however, is done before the quilt is quilted. Place the right sides of the quilt top and backing together over the batting, and stitch around the outside edges, leaving an opening through which the quilt is turned. Then slip stitch the opening closed.

Preparation for Quilting

Decide what designs you want to make with the quilting stitches. For a traditional look, outline important elements of the design with quilting. A grid of stitching works well in background areas. Fancier design elements that complement the theme of the quilt can also be incorporated. Make sure that there will be some stitching every few inches to secure the batting so it doesn't shift.

Decide now if you need to mark the top for quilting. Mark simple outlining or grids with masking tape as you quilt. For more elaborate quilting designs, mark the top with one of the marking tools described on page 199. Use the lightest mark possible. Dark marks may be difficult to remove when the quilt is finished.

Spread out the backing (right side down) on a table or other flat surface. Use masking tape to secure it after smoothing it out. Place the batting on top of the backing, smoothing it out also. Finally, place the completed quilt top on the backing, right side up. Stretch it out so it is smooth, and tape it.

For hand quilting, baste the layers together using long stitches. For best results, start basting at the center of the quilt and work toward the edges. Create a grid of basting by making a line of stitching approximately every 4 inches.

For machine quilting, baste by hand as described above or use safety pins. Place a safety pin every 3 or 4 inches. To save time later, avoid placing pins on quilting lines.

QUILTING

Quilting, stitching that goes through all three layers of the quilt, is both functional and decorative. It holds the batting in place. It is also an important design element, greatly enhancing the texture of the finished quilt. Hand quilting has a beautiful, classic appearance that can't be duplicated, but it requires much more time than machine quilting. Machine quilting can be more dramatic because the tension of the stitches tends to create more extreme peaks and valleys. It is much faster to create, and it wears well.

To outline design areas, stitch ¼ inch away from each seam line. Simply decide where to stitch by eye or use ¼-inch masking tape placed along each seam as a guide. Masking tape can also be used as guides for straight lines and grids. Stitch beside the edge of the tape, avoiding stitching through the tape and getting the adhesive on the needle and thread. After you're finished quilting for the day, do not leave the masking tape on the fabric; it can leave a sticky residue that is difficult to remove.

Hand Quilting

Some quilters hold their work unsupported in their lap when they quilt. Most quilters, however, prefer to use some sort of quilting hoop or frame to hold the quilt stretched out. This makes it easier to stitch with an even tension and helps prevent puckering and tucks.

Use betweens (quilting needles) for hand quilting. The smaller the needle (higher numbers such as 11 and 12), the easier it will be to make small stitches. A quilting thimble on the third finger of your quilting hand will protect you from needle sores.

Use no more than 18 inches of quilting thread. Longer thread tends to tangle, and the end gets worn as it is pulled through the fabric. Knot the end of the thread with a quilter's knot. Slip the needle into the quilt top and batting about an inch from where the first stitch should start. Pull the needle up through the quilt top at the beginning of the first stitch. Hold the thread firmly and give it a little tug. The knot should pop into the batting and lodge between the quilt top and the backing.

The quilting stitch is a running stitch. Place your free hand (left hand for right-handed people) under the quilt to feel for the needle as it pokes through the back. Load the needle with a few stitches by rocking the needle back and forth. Focus on making even stitches, but make sure you go through all three layers. When you have mastered that, work on making the stitches smaller on future quilts.

Machine Quilting

Machine quilting is easy to learn, but it does take some practice. Make a few trial runs before starting to stitch on your completed quilt. On the test swatch, adjust the tension settings for the machine so that the stitches are even and do not pucker or have loose loops of thread.

The easiest machine stitching is long straight lines, starting at the center of the quilt and radiating out. These lines may be in a grid, stitched in the ditches formed by the seams, outlines around design elements, or channels (long, evenly spaced lines). Whatever the pattern, quilt from the center to the outer edges. Plan the order of stitching to minimize the need to start and stop.

Before placing the quilt on the sewing machine, roll the sides in toward the center, and secure the rolls with pins or bicycle clips. Use an even-feed walking foot for straight lines of stitching. For freehand stitching, use a darning foot and lower the feed dogs or use a throat plate that covers the feed dogs.

To begin, turn the handwheel to lower and raise the needle to its highest point. Pull gently on the top thread to bring the bobbin thread up through the quilt. Stitch in place for several stitches. Gradually increase the length of each stitch for the first ½ inch of quilting until the stitches are the desired length. This will secure the ends of the threads making it unnecessary to backstitch or make knots. Reverse these steps at the end of each line of quilting.

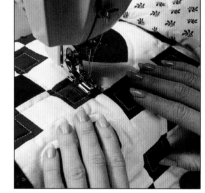

When quilting with the even-feed walking foot, place your hands on either side of the pressure foot and apply even pressure. Keep the layers smooth and free of tucks.

During freehand quilting, place your hands around the darning foot and apply gentle outward pressure to keep the layers smooth. Guide the fabric with smooth, even motions of the wrist. In freehand quilting, the fabric is free to move in any direction; it is not fed through the machine by the

feed dogs. The stitch length is determined by the speed of the needle and the motion of the fabric under the needle. To keep the stitches the same length, maintain a steady speed and even motion. It takes some practice to get smooth curves and even stitch lengths using this technique. Don't be discouraged if your first attempts are a bit rough.

Tying Quilts

The fastest way to secure the layers of a quilt (top, batting, and backing) together is to tie them. Thread a needle with a long piece of embroidery floss, yarn, or pearl cotton. At regular intervals (every 4 inches, at most) take a single stitch through the  three layers of quilt. Tie the thread in a double square knot, and trim the thread to a consistent length, usually ½ inch.

 If you prefer, you can tie your quilt by machine. Baste as usual. Place the quilt on the machine and make sure all the layers are smooth. Set the stitch length and width to 0. Take several stitches and then increase the stitch width to a wide setting. Make about eight stitches and return the stitch width to 0. Make several stitches, and clip the threads. Repeat until the quilt is tied at regular intervals.

To make the ties more decorative, use a decorative stitch instead of the zigzag stitch.

BINDING

Binding may be made from strips of fabric that match or coordinate with the fabrics used in the quilt. These strips may be cut on the straight grain or on the bias. Straight binding is easier to cut and apply. Quilts that have curved edges require bias binding. Also, bias binding is stronger and tends to last longer. You can purchase quilt binding. Apply according to the manufacturer's instructions.

To make straight binding, cut strips of fabric 3¼ inches wide on the lengthwise or crosswise grain. For each side of the quilt, you will need a strip the length of that side plus 2 inches. For example, if the side measures 40 inches long, cut your strips 42 inches long.

Baste around the quilt, ¼ inch from the outer edge. Make sure all corners are square, and trim any excess batting or fabric. Prepare each strip of binding by folding it in half lengthwise, wrong sides together, and press. Find the center of each strip. Also find the center of each side of the quilt.

Place the binding strip on top of the quilt, aligning the raw edges of the strip and the quilt and matching the centers. Stitch a ½-inch seam from one end of the quilt to the other. If you use an even-feed walking foot, it will be easier to keep the binding and the quilt smooth.

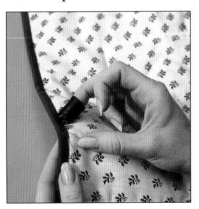 Trim the excess binding from each end. Fold the binding to the back of the quilt and slip stitch it in place. Repeat for the other sides of the quilt. Attach the binding to the ends of the quilt using the same procedure except *do not* trim the ends of the binding. Instead, fold the excess binding over the end of the quilt. Holding the end in place, fold the binding to the back of the quilt and slip stitch in place.

Blocks and Borders Index

A

Album Block, 128
Apple Cider, 88
Apple Pie, 80
Appliqué
    Apple Cider, 88
    Apple Pie, 80
    Attic Window, 76
    Bloom Well Groomed, 168
    Borrow and Return, 44
    Cherry Basket, 78
    Crazy Patch, 40
    Cupid's Own, 38
    Double Heart, 74
    Emily's Heart, 32
    Flowers and More, 179
    Fly Away Ladybug!, 152
    Flying High, 142
    Garden Queen Iris, 164
    Good Morning Glory, 166
    Gossamer Wings, 162
    Grandma's Bowls, 82
    Heart Can, 72
    Hearts, 187
    Heart's Delight, 42
    Home Sweet Home, 62
    Honey Pot, 60
    Johnny-Jump-Ups, 158
    Peeping Out, 154
    Pretty Maids, 148
    Pride of the Bride, 28
    Rambling Leaves, 177
    Rooster, 70
    Shooting Star, 18
    Sweet Clover, 14
    Sweet Nectar, 144
    Teapot, 54
    Watering Can, 136
    Watermelon, 52
    Wayward Daisy, 134
Attic Window, 76

B

Bars and Blocks, 189
Basket, 126
Birdhouse Treasure, 170
Block Leaf, 176
Blocks and Bars, 180
Bloom Well Groomed, 168
Borrow and Return, 44
Braided, 193
Bricks, 181

A

Card Trick, 124
Chain (variation), 122
Cherry Basket, 78
Chimneys and Cornerstones, 86
Chinese Fan, 120
Churn Dash, 68
Churn Dash, 188
City Streets, 84
Crazy Patch, 40
Cross, 116
Cupid's Own, 38

D

Diamond Star, 36
Diamond Star Squares, 190
Double Heart, 74
Double Picture Frame, 178
Double Pinwheel, 114
Double T, 34

E

Eight-Pointed Star, 46
Eight-Pointed Star, 194
Emily's Heart, 32

F

Flowers and More, 179
Fluttering by Butterfly, 160
Fly Away Ladybug!, 152
Flying Geese, 184
Flying Geese (variation), 112
Flying High, 142
Four Corner Flowers, 110

Friendship Circle, 118
Friendship Star, 30
Friendship Star (variation), 108

G

Garden of Eden, 64
Garden Queen Iris, 164
Girl's Joy, 26
Good Morning Glory, 166
Gossamer Wings, 162
Grandma's Bowls, 82

H

Handweave, 58
Heart Can, 72
Hearts, 187
Heart's Delight, 42
Heart Wreath, 24
Home Sweet Home, 62
Honey Pot, 60
Hourglass, 66

I

Inching Along, 156

J

Jagged Edge, 191
Johnny-Jump-Ups, 158
Judy in Arabia, 22

K

Kaleidoscope, 106

L

Log Cabin, 104
London Square, 102

M

My Favorite Flower, 150

O

Ohio Snowflake, 20
Ohio Star, 100

P

Palm Tree, 98
Peeping Out, 154
Piano Keys, 182

Note: Borders are italic.

Pieced
    Album Block, 128
    Attic Window, 76
    Bars and Blocks, 189
    Basket, 126
    Birdhouse Treasure, 170
    Block Leaf, 176
    Blocks and Bars, 180
    Borrow and Return, 44
    Braided, 193
    Bricks, 181
    Card Trick, 124
    Chain (variation), 122
    Chimneys and Cornerstones, 86
    Chinese Fan, 120
    Churn Dash, 68
    Churn Dash, 188
    City Streets, 84
    Crazy Patch, 40
    Cross, 116
    Cupid's Own, 38
    Diamond Star, 36
    Diamond Star Squares, 190
    Double Heart, 74
    Double Picture Frame, 178
    Double Pinwheel, 114
    Double T, 34
    Eight-Pointed Star, 46
    Eight-Pointed Star, 194
    Emily's Heart, 32
    Fluttering by Butterfly, 160
    Flying Geese, 184
    Flying Geese (variation), 112
    Four Corner Flowers, 110
    Friendship Circle, 118
    Friendship Star, 30
    Friendship Star (variation), 108
    Garden of Eden, 64
    Girl's Joy, 26
    Handweave, 58

    Heart's Delight, 42
    Heart Wreath, 24
    Hourglass, 66
    Inching Along, 156
    Jagged Edge, 191
    Judy in Arabia, 22
    Kaleidoscope, 106
    Log Cabin, 104
    London Square, 102
    My Favorite Flower, 150
    Ohio Snowflake, 20
    Ohio Star, 100
    Palm Tree, 98
    Piano Keys, 182
    Pretty Bird, 172
    Pride of the Bride, 28
    Rail Fence, 130
    Rickrack, 183
    Sawtooth Square, 192
    Scalloped, 185
    Square upon Square, 96
    Stained Glass, 94
    Stop Sign, 186
    Summer Sunflower, 146
    Sun Rays, 16
    Sunshine Day, 140
    Sweet Clover, 14
    Traditional Fan, 92
    Triangles, 195
    True Lover's Knot, 12
    Trumpeting Tulip, 138
    Twelve Triangles, 56
    Twisted Star, 10
    Virginia Reel, 8
    Watermelon, 52
    Windblown Puzzle, 50
Pretty Bird, 172
Pretty Maids, 148
Pride of the Bride, 28

R
Rail Fence, 130
Rambling Leaves, 177
Rickrack, 183
Rooster, 70

S
Sawtooth Square, 192
Scalloped, 185
Shooting Star, 18
Square upon Square, 96
Stained Glass, 94
Stop Sign, 186
Summer Sunflower, 146
Sun Rays, 16
Sunshine Day, 140
Sweet Clover, 14
Sweet Nectar, 144

T
Teapot, 54
Traditional Fan, 92
Triangles, 195
True Lover's Knot, 12
Trumpeting Tulip, 138
Twelve Triangles, 56
Twisted Star, 10

V
Virginia Reel, 8

W
Watering Can, 136
Watermelon, 52
Wayward Daisy, 134
Windblown Puzzle, 50

Resource Directory

DESIGNERS

Phyllis Dobbs
Phyllis Dobbs Design Studio
220 Marwood Circle
Birmingham, AL 35244
Phone: 205-991-3065
www.phyllisdobbs.com

Mimi Shimp
Quiltime
9640 Tropical Parkway
Las Vegas, NV 89149
Phone: 702-658-7988
Fax: 702-658-7133
www.quiltime.com
E-mail: mimi@quiltime.com

Lucie Sinkler
Close Knit, Inc.
622 Grove Street
Evanston, IL 60201
Phone: 847-328-6760

Retta Warehime
Sew Cherished
South 2630 Kellogg
Kennewick, WA 99338
Phone: 509-783-2795

FABRICS

Benartex, Inc.
1359 Broadway
Suite 1100
New York, NY 10018
Phone 212-840-3250
www.benartex.com
E-mail: info@benartex.com

Cranston Village
2 Worcester Road
Webster, MA 01570
Phone: 800-876-2756
www.CranstonVillage.com

FreeSpirit Fabric
1350 Broadway
21st Floor
New York, NY 10018
www.freespiritfabric.com
E-mail: information@freespiritfabric.com

Hancock Fabrics, Inc.
One Fashion Way
Baldwyn, MS 38824
Phone: 877-322-7427
www.hancockfabrics.com
The Fresh from the Garden quilt is made from Hancock Fabrics's Flannel Whimsy line designed by Phyllis Dobbs.

Marcus Brothers Textiles, Inc.
980 Avenue of the Americas
New York, NY 10018
Phone: 212-354-8700
Fax: 212-354-5245
www.marcusbrothers.com

Moda Fabrics/United Notions
13795 Hutton Drive
Dallas, TX 75234
Phone: 800-527-9447
Fax: 800-468-4209
www.modafabrics.com
The Country Cupboard quilt is made from Moda Fabrics's Gingham Rose line.

P&B Textiles
1580 Gilbreth Road
Burlingame, CA 94010
www.pbtex.com

Red Rooster Fabrics
1359 Broadway
Suite 1202
New York, NY 10018
Phone: 212-244-6596
Fax: 212-760-1536

Timeless Treasures Fabrics, Inc.
483 Broadway
New York, NY 10013
Phone: 212-226-1400
Fax: 212-925-4180
www.ttfabrics.com

SUPPLIES

Coats & Clark
Consumer Services
P.O. Box 12229
Greenville, SC 29612-0229
Phone: 800-648-1479
www.coatsandclark.com

The DMC Corporation
Hackensack Avenue
Kearny, NJ 07032-4689
Phone: 973-589-0606
www.dmc-usa.com

Janome America, Inc.
10 Industrial Avenue
Mahwah, NJ 07430
Phone: 201-825-3200
Fax: 201-825-3612
www.janome.com

J.T. Trading Corporation
3 Simm Lane
Newtown, CT 06470
Phone: 203-270-774
www.sprayandfix.com

Quiltime
9640 Tropical Parkway
Las Vegas, NV 89149
Phone: 702-658-7988
Fax: 702-658-7133
www.quiltime.com

Superior Threads
P.O. Box 1672
St. George, UT 84771
Phone: 800-499-1777
Fax: 435-628-6385
www.superiorthreads.com
E-mail: info@superiorthreads.com

The Warm Company
954 East Union Street
Seattle, WA 98122
Phone: 206-320-9276
Fax: 206-320-0974
www.warmcompany.com
E-mail: info@warmcompany.com

QUILTING SERVICES

Leta Brazell
Quilts from the Heart
417 Tramway NE
Albuquerque, NM 87123
Phone: 505-292-8560